Israeli A

'This book deals rationally and cogently with a topic that almost always generates considerable heat even just with book titles. The reader may not agree with everything that White asserts but it is a highly commendable effort to throw light on a fraught subject.'

Archbishop Desmond Tutu, Nobel Peace Prize Laureate

'A very strong and clear voice that does not shun from exposing in full, and in a most accessible manner, the essence of Zionism and Israeli policies in Palestine. In a world confused by competing narratives, disinformation and fabrication, this book is an excellent guide for understanding the magnitude of the crimes committed against the Palestinians and the nature of their present suffering and oppression.'

Professor Ilan Pappe, University of Exeter, Israeli historian and author of *The Ethnic Cleansing of Palestine* (2007)

'This book provides one of the best introductions to the Israel/Palestine conflict. It reveals what mainstream media in the West seeks to conceal from the public: that Israel has an apartheid regime which has been obsessed with demographic racism and ethnic cleansing for six decades. The book provides an indispensable context for understanding the origins and consequences of the conflict. It also makes by far the most compelling case for 'peace with justice-not apartheid'.'

Nur Masalha, Reader in Religion and Politics, St Mary's University College (UK), and author of *The Bible and Zionism* (2007)

'Is Israel an apartheid state? The answer to this question has enormous implications for how states and international civil society should act towards a country that bills itself as the moral guardian of the memory and lessons of the Nazi Holocaust – that is why it is so heavily contested. But there is no doubt that Israel is constituted as a "Jewish state". The problem is that half the population it controls – the indigenous Palestinians – is not Jewish. In this carefully researched book, Ben White demonstrates that indeed Israel could have become and could not continue to be a "Jewish state" unless it used discriminatory tactics that resemble and often surpass those of apartheid South Africa. At a time when Israel appears to regard any action against Palestine's indigenous people – no matter how violent and illegal – as justified, this book is essential reading for those who want to deepen their understanding beyond soundbites and spin.'

Ali Abunimah, Co-founder of Electronic Intifada,
author of *One Country* (2007)

'Ben White's new book *Israeli Apartheid: A Beginner's Guide* is a useful introduction to a vital debate. To understand the challenges of the current situation in the Middle East we must revisit the long and often painful journey that led from the creation of Israel to the 40-year long occupation of the Palestinians. This challenging new work unpicks some of the myths of that story and forces us all to look again at the reality of current Israeli policy towards the Palestinians.'

Crispin Blunt, Conservative Member of Parliament for Reigate

'There are always those who say the conflict in Palestine is too complicated for anyone to dare engage with it, much less understand it. Yet here is the book which answers them, and it does so with a rare intelligence and fine line of argument. Drawn from a rich range of sources, Ben White's *Israeli Apartheid: A Beginner's Guide* takes on the most complex arenas of injustice and contested history, and renders them accessible, lucid, and morally compelling. Never compromising on the facts, its narrative both enlightens and inspires. If you want to learn about Palestine, start here.'

Karma Nabulsi, Oxford University academic

'An essential guide for understanding the reality of Israeli apartheid – both the history, and the day to day reality.'

Eyal Weizman, Israeli architect and author of
Hollow Land: Israel's Architecture of Occupation (2007)

'I am impressed by Ben White's clear-minded journalism and analysis. I have quoted from an article of his in a speech to The House of Commons. I feel sure his book will be of value in understanding the attitudes behind the Middle East division.'

Harry Cohen, Labour Member of Parliament
for Leyton and Wanstead

'White's book helps us see much more clearly both what is happening in Israel/Palestine but also what we must do about it. If you really care about peace in the Middle East, read this book. Then commit yourself to supporting non-violent proactive ways to bring justice with peace for both Israelis and Palestinians.'

Rev. Stephen Sizer, author of *Zion's Christian Soldiers* (2007)

'Ben White provides a lucid and essential account of the roots, nature and development of Israeli apartheid and the continued resistance – home grown or international. His work cleverly unites the relevant past to the unbearable present, and provides a solid presentation of the ongoing struggle to rid the Zionist state of its racially selective "democracy". His writing is dispassionate, clear and thoroughly substantiated, as is the case with all of his work.'

Ramzy Baroud, editor of the *Palestine Chronicle* website,
journalist and author of *The Second Palestinian Intifada* (2006)

'Ben White presents a book to be used and not only read. It is to be used by all those who are interested in taking a political and historic journey into the Palestinian-Israeli conflict and who are involved in moving beyond the historic narratives into creating a future where peace prevails in the Middle East.'

Sami Awad, Executive Director of Holy Land Trust,
Bethlehem, Palestine

'This is not a story for the faint of heart but it is a necessary story, rarely told with such candour. This is also one of those rare books that will permanently change a reader's view of the world and inevitably force us to ask about our own country's complicity in this occupation.'

Gary M. Burge, PhD, Wheaton College and Graduate School,
author of *Whose Land? Whose Promise?* (2003)

Israeli Apartheid

A Beginner's Guide

Ben White

PLUTO PRESS
www.plutobooks.com

First published 2009 by Pluto Press
345 Archway Road, London N6 5AA and
175 Fifth Avenue, New York, NY 10010

www.plutobooks.com

Distributed in the United States of America exclusively by
Palgrave Macmillan, a division of St. Martin's Press LLC,
175 Fifth Avenue, New York, NY 10010

British Library Cataloguing in Publication Data

A catalogue record for this book is available from the British Library

ISBN   978 0 7453 2888 1   Hardback
ISBN   978 0 7453 2887 4   Paperback

Library of Congress Cataloging in Publication Data applied for

This book is printed on paper suitable for recycling and made from
fully managed and sustained forest sources. Logging, pulping and
manufacturing processes are expected to conform to the environmental
standards of the country of origin. The paper may contain up to
70 per cent post-consumer waste.

10   9   8   7   6   5   4   3   2   1

Designed and produced for Pluto Press by
Chase Publishing Services Ltd, Sidmouth, England
Typeset from disk by Stanford DTP Services, Northampton, England
Printed and bound in the European Union by
CPI Antony Rowe, Chippenham and Eastbourne

إلى الصامدين

To the steadfast ones

Contents

Maps, Charts and Photographs

Acknowledgements

A lot of people have worked hard to make this book what it is, and for that I am very grateful. I cannot thank everyone here as much as I would like, and there are many dear friends and family who helped simply with their friendship and support. An especial thanks though to the following who gave invaluable assistance, advice and encouragement:

Roger van Zwanenberg and all the team at Pluto Press – particularly Robert Webb.

Andy Sims, Alex Awad, Lizzie Clifford, Jonathan Cook, Ilan Pappe, Khaled Hroub, Glen Rangwala, Jonathan Kuttab, Arthur Nelsen, Suhad Bishara at Adalah; John Dugard, Paul Higgins, Penny Julian, Karma Nabulsi, Isabelle Humphries, Ramzy Baroud and the *Palestine Chronicle*; Philip Rizk, Colin Chapman, Washington Report on Middle East Affairs (WRMEA); Daoud Badr at the Association for the Defense of the Rights of Internally Displaced Persons in Israel (ADRID); Stephen Sizer, Shaza Younis, Daoud Nassar, Institute for Middle East Understanding (IMEU); Professor Gary Burge, Juliette Bannoura at the Applied Research Institute of Jerusalem (ARIJ); Muzna Shihabi and Ashraf Khatib at the Negotiations Affairs Department; the Palestinian Academic Society for the Study of International Affairs (PASSIA); Waseem Mardini and the Foundation for Middle East Peace (FMEP); Amnesty International; the United Nations Office for the Coordination of Humanitarian Affairs in the OPT (OCHA); and Sami Mshasha at the United Nations Relief and Works Agency for Palestine Refugees in the Near East (UNRWA), Jerusalem.

Foreword

John Dugard

Perhaps the most striking aspect of the Israel/Palestine conflict is that it is so little discussed in the West, particularly in the United States. Unlike the human rights situation in Zimbabwe, Sudan, Burma, Tibet and Cuba it is a taboo topic in most quarters. Whereas human rights in apartheid South Africa was vigorously debated in the media, universities, churches, shareholders meetings and social and professional gatherings the subject of human rights in the Occupied Palestinian Territory (OPT) is studiously avoided. This contrasts with the position in Israel itself, where all issues are examined and debated in the media and public life. As Special Rapporteur to the Human Rights Council (previously Commission for Human Rights) on the Human Rights Situation in the OPT, I spoke in Israel to the Knesset on house demolitions, at the Hebrew University of Jerusalem on human rights violations in the OPT and at other meetings on controversial aspects of the conflict. But in the West one is not so welcome to express opinions on this subject. It seems that one can address real issues in Israel itself without the risk of being labelled as anti-Semitic but in the West it is not so. In many quarters any frank criticism of Israel's treatment of the Palestinians is viewed as anti-Semitic.

The failure to discuss and debate the conflict presents a serious problem as until it is fully aired the conflict will not be resolved. Herein lies the value of the present work. Unlike the many available comprehensive and scholarly studies of the conflict which inevitably have a limited readership, this book highlights the key issues of the conflict in a short and highly readable study, in which brevity is not achieved at the expense of a serious analysis of Israeli law and practice or a proper treatment of the historical record. All the principal topics at the heart of the conflict are addressed: the treatment of Palestinians both within Israel itself and the OPT, why Palestinians reject the notion of a 'Jewish state', is Israel a democracy, is Gaza still occupied by Israel, the plight of Palestinian refugees, the expansion of settlements, the Wall presently being constructed in the OPT, checkpoints etc., etc. In short the book is an ideal reader for informed debate about the conflict.

Many will take issue with the comparison with apartheid. Ben White does not, however, say that apartheid and Israel's treatment of Palestinians are exactly the same. What he says is that they have certain similarities, that they resemble each other. That is why he calls it Israeli apartheid. It is Israel's own version of a system that has been universally condemned. Of course there are differences, as White freely admits. Apartheid in South Africa was a regime of institutionalised race discrimination in which a white minority sought to maintain domination over a black majority, whereas Israeli apartheid is concerned with the discriminatory treatment of a minority of Palestinians in Israel itself and the discriminatory treatment of Palestinians in the OPT under a regime of military occupation that, unlike apartheid, is tolerated by international law. But, as White points out, there are similarities. He rightly says that 'The common element of both legal systems is the intention to consolidate and enforce dispossession, securing the best land control over natural resources for one group at the expense of another.' Control is achieved in Israel/Palestine by many of the same devices employed in apartheid South Africa: colonisation or the settlement of land owned by the indigenous population; territorial fragmentation of the OPT by a process of Bantustanisation; restrictions on movement by a strict system of permits and checkpoints that brings to mind the much-hated pass system of apartheid, but probably exceeds the pass system in severity; house demolitions, military brutality and the arrest and imprisonment of political opponents. Control is also achieved by means not employed by the apartheid regime: a wall/fence/barrier (whatever you like to call it) that divides and separates people; a system of separate and unequal roads for Israelis (who get the best roads) and Palestinians (who get the poor roads); and a deliberately manufactured humanitarian crisis that has reduced the Palestinian people to a state of poverty and despair. This last difference is perhaps the most striking. Whereas the Israeli military occupation of the OPT has resulted in the destruction of houses, agriculture and businesses, the impairment of schools, universities, hospitals and clinics, damage to electricity plants, water supplies and other amenities, and the subjection of the Palestinian people to poverty, the apartheid state, in order to promote a pretence of equal treatment, built houses, schools, universities, businesses, hospitals, clinics and provided water to the black population. It sought to advance the material welfare of the black people while denying political rights. Israel, on the other hand, denies political rights to Palestinians and at the same time undermines their material welfare – in violation of its obligations as an occupying power under international humanitarian law.

Israel has been condemned for its policies in the OPT by numerous United Nations resolutions and by the International

Court of Justice, in an advisory opinion of 2004 in which it held that the wall Israel is constructing in Palestinian Territory is illegal and should be dismantled. But no serious attempt is made by the West to compel Israel to comply with its international obligations. As White correctly states 'Israel has been exempted from sanction for breaking international legal norms.' In this respect the response of the international community differs substantially from its response to apartheid. The General Assembly of the United Nations called for widespread economic sanctions on South Africa, the Security Council imposed a mandatory arms embargo, every effort was made to compel South Africa to comply with an advisory opinion of the International Court of Justice condemning apartheid in Namibia, and states, corporations and civil society imposed various forms of sanctions. This too is an issue that must be addressed if the credibility of the Rule of Law is to be maintained.

Ben White's book is no stranger to controversy. It considers issues that many in the West would like to see swept under the carpet. But the Palestinian issue is one that threatens international peace and cannot be avoided. The present book, by presenting the issues that need to be considered in a readable, but highly informative, manner will, it is hoped, stimulate an awareness of the plight of the Palestinian people. Until this is fully understood and appreciated a just settlement of the conflict will remain as elusive as ever.

John Dugard

Professor of Law, Centre for Human Rights, University of Pretoria; Visiting Professor of Law, Duke University, North Carolina; Former Special Rapporteur to the Human Rights Council on the Human Rights Situation in the Occupied Palestinian Territory.

Map 1   General map of Palestine/Israel

Source: Keith Cook, in Jonathan Cook, *Blood and Religion*, London: Pluto, p. xv.

Introducing Israeli Apartheid

Supporters of Israel present Zionism as an ideology of liberation of the Jewish people, but for Palestinians, Zionism, as it has been practiced and as they have experienced it, has been precisely apartheid.[1]

Approaching the Israeli-Palestinian conflict for the first time can be a confusing experience. There seem to be such widely varying points of view, contradictory versions of history, and utterly opposing explanations for the root of the problem. Why is this? One of the main reasons for this difficulty is the fact there are disagreements over Israel's origins.

In this book, the truth of Israel's past and present is laid bare; the ethnic cleansing, land grabs, discriminatory legislation and military occupation. This reality is very different from the typical tale of a small, brave nation, forced from the very beginning to fight for survival against implacable, bloodthirsty enemies; a country that has made mistakes but has always done its best to achieve noble aims with pure means.

What can explain such a profound difference? Pro-Israeli propaganda in the West has had a huge impact, but there is a more fundamental reason. 'Security' has been the justification for all manner of Israeli policies, from the population expulsions in 1948, to the Separation Wall over 60 years later. Defence, so it goes, is why Israel is forced to take certain measures, however unpleasant they may be.

Indeed, Israel argues, it alone is a country that fights for its very survival. Even putting aside Israel's vast military strength, why would Israel's existence as a Jewish state be so objectionable to Palestinians? Unlike today's slick apologists, the early Zionists were refreshingly honest about the reality of their mission, as we will see more of in Part I.

Ze'ev Jabotinsky was one of the foremost Zionist leaders and theoreticians, a man who has more streets in Israel named in his honour than any other historical figure.[2] In perhaps his most famous essay written in 1923, Jabotinsky was clear about one thing: 'Zionist colonization, even the most restricted, must either be terminated or carried out in defiance of the will of the native population'.[3] Why? Simply put, history shows that 'every indigenous people will resist alien settlers'.[4]

This book has been written in order to describe clearly and simply what Zionism has meant for the Palestinians, how Israeli apartheid has been implemented and maintained, and suggestions for how it can be resisted. In this task, I am indebted to the many academics, writers and journalists who have researched, documented and witnessed the unfolding of Israeli apartheid in Palestine.

Part I begins with a concise history of the development of Zionist settlement and theory, particularly with how it related to the Palestinians. There is then a summary of the key historical events of the Nakba, the Palestinian Catastrophe of 1948, when the aim of a Jewish state in Palestine was realised.

Part II will clearly define the main areas of Israeli apartheid and the contradictions of a so-called 'Jewish democratic' state. Dispersed through Parts I and II will be small 'stand alone' boxes with personal stories of how individual Palestinians are affected by a given aspect of Israeli apartheid.

Part III is the section in which ways to resist Israeli apartheid are discussed, with details of existing initiatives that should hopefully encourage you the reader to think of your own ideas. Finally, the book concludes with a 'Frequently Asked Questions' section in which doubts or criticisms of the book's main thrust will be asked and answered. But first, we are going to take a look at the definition of apartheid in international law, and the similarities and differences between South African apartheid and Israel.

DEFINING APARTHEID

For the purpose of the present Convention, the term 'the crime of apartheid', which shall include similar policies and practices of racial segregation and discrimination as practised in southern Africa, shall apply to the following inhuman acts *committed for the purpose of establishing and maintaining domination by one racial group of persons over any other racial group of persons and systematically oppressing them...*[5] [emphasis added]

Article II, International Convention on the Suppression and Punishment of the Crime of Apartheid, UN General Assembly Resolution 3068, 30 November 1973

While South Africa is most associated with apartheid (and is the context from which the term originates), the crime of apartheid actually has a far broader definition. This is important in the case of Israel, since even putting aside the similarities and differences to the South Africa case specifically, we have some kind of measure by which to assess Israel's policies past and present towards the Palestinians.

In 1973, the UN's General Assembly adopted the International Convention on the Suppression and Punishment of the Crime of Apartheid, which meant agreeing on a detailed description of what exactly 'the crime of apartheid' looked like. From this list of 'inhuman acts', there are some particularly worth highlighting:

- Denial to a member or members of a racial group or groups of the right to life and liberty of person ... by the infliction upon the members of a racial group or groups of serious bodily or mental harm, by the infringement of their freedom or dignity, or by subjecting them to torture or to cruel, inhuman or degrading treatment or punishment.
- Any legislative measures and other measures calculated to prevent a racial group or groups from participation in the political, social, economic and cultural life of the country ... [including] the right to leave and to return to their country, the right to a nationality, the right to freedom of movement and residence ...
- Any measures including legislative measures designed to divide the population along racial lines by the creation of separate reserves and ghettos for the members of a racial group or groups ... the expropriation of landed property belonging to a racial group ...

As will be described in Parts I and II of this book, Israel has been, and continues to be, guilty of these crimes, which are all the more serious for having been 'committed for the purpose of establishing and maintaining domination by one racial group of persons over any other racial group of persons'.

More recently, the Rome Statute of the International Criminal Court (ICC) was adopted in 1998 at an international conference.[6] Israel was actually one of seven countries (out of 148) to vote against the statute. The ICC Statute includes the 'crime of apartheid' in a list of 'crimes against humanity', going on to describe apartheid as:

> inhumane acts ... committed in the context of an institutionalized regime of systematic oppression and domination by one racial group over any other racial group or groups and committed with the intention of maintaining that regime ...

Therefore, even before a consideration of the similarities and differences between Israel and apartheid South Africa, there is a clear set of criteria for what constitutes the crime of apartheid under international law with which we can assess Israel's policies since 1948.

THE SOUTH AFRICA COMPARISON

> If Palestinians were black, Israel would now be a pariah state subject to economic sanctions led by the United States.[7]
>
> Observer, October 2000

> White settlers in South Africa, like Zionist pioneers, colonised a land already inhabited. As in South Africa, the settlers in Palestine expelled the indigenous population, some two-thirds of the Palestinians in the land that became Israel in 1948, took possession of their properties and legally segregated those who remained.[8]

> It seems to me that the Israelis would like the Palestinians to disappear. There was never anything like that in our case. The whites did not want the blacks to disappear.[9]
>
> Mondli Makhanya, editor-in-chief of the
> South African Sunday Times, July 2008

Israel was compared to South African apartheid long before Jimmy Carter wrote his bestseller 'Peace not Apartheid'. While the legal infrastructure that enforced apartheid South Africa differs substantially from the relevant Israeli legislation, there are also strong similarities.[10] The common element of both legal systems is the intention to consolidate and enforce dispossession, securing the best land control over natural resources for one group at the expense of another.

Architect and academic Lindsay Bremner has observed that while in the popular imagination apartheid in South Africa meant walls, fences and barbed wire separating blacks and whites, in fact:

> it was the countless instruments of control and humiliation (racially discriminatory laws, administration boards, commissions of inquiry, town planning schemes, health regulations, pass books, spot fines, location permits, police raids, removal vans, bulldozers) ... that delineated South African society during the apartheid years and produced its characteristic landscapes.[11]

As will be seen in Part II, this kind of description is all too familiar for Palestinians inside Israel, and the OPT, for whom – like black South Africans – 'daily acts and rituals' become 'acts of segregation and humiliation'.[12]

In a bitter irony, important parts of the so-called 'peace process' of the 1990s, which saw limited Palestinian 'self rule' in a small percentage of the OPT, have actually strengthened the comparison with apartheid South Africa. In 1959, South Africa passed a law designed to promote 'self-government' amongst blacks in sealed-off 'reservations'.[13] Reading this description by the late Israeli journalist Tanya Reinhart, the similarities with the situation in the OPT since the 1990s are striking:

The power in each of these entities was bestowed to local flunkies, and a few Bantustans even had elections, Parliaments, and quasi-governmental institutions ... The Bantustans were allowed some symbols of sovereignty: a flag, postage stamps, passports and strong police force.

In 1984, Desmond Tutu noted that the Bantustans, in territory 'arbitrarily carved up for them by the all mighty White Government' deprived of 'territorial integrity or any hope of economic viability' were basically intended to 'give a semblance of morality to something that had been condemned as evil'.[14] 'Fragmented and discontinuous territories, located in unproductive and marginal parts of the country' with 'no control' over natural resources or access to 'territorial waters' – as we shall see, this is a frighteningly spot-on description of the OPT today.[15]

However, to describe Israel as an apartheid state 'does not mean equating 'Israel with South Africa'.[16] Indeed, any comparison should highlight both 'corresponding developments' as well as 'obviously different circumstances'.[17] One particularly striking difference is the fact that the apartheid regime in South Africa meant the rule of a white minority over a sizeable black majority; in 1913, when 'the first segregation laws were passed', the indigenous blacks made up 'more than 75% of the total labour force'.[18]

The other main difference is that Israel has not practised so-called 'petty' apartheid – in other words, there are no public toilets marked 'Jews' and 'Non-Jews'. Palestinian citizens of Israel have full voting rights and there are a small number of elected Palestinians in the Israeli legislature (the Knesset). This is because had the 'discrimination against Palestinians been written into Israeli law as specifically as discrimination against Blacks' was written into South African law, then 'outside support would surely be jeopardized'.[19]

There is one key difference between Israel and apartheid South Africa that Zionists definitely do not trumpet. While in apartheid South Africa, the settlers 'exploited' the 'labour power' of the dispossessed natives, in the case of Israel, 'the native population was to be eliminated; exterminated or expelled rather than exploited'.[20] It could be said that Zionism has been *worse* for the indigenous population than apartheid was in South Africa – Israel needs the land, but without the people.

In a conversation between Israeli historian Benny Morris and Palestinian American academic Joseph Massad, the latter compared Israel to South Africa by way of its 'supremacist rights'.[21] Morris said this was 'ridiculous', responding that throughout Zionism's history, Zionists 'would have much preferred Palestine to be empty of Arabs with therefore no need for Jews to be supreme over anybody. They simply wanted a Jewish state.'

Morris's objection to the term 'supremacist' is revealing, as it flags up the problem that has haunted Zionism until today. South African apartheid had a critical internal contradiction: while aiming 'at setting racial groups apart', it also 'acknowledged their dependency'.[22] Zionism, on the other hand, has tried 'disappearing' the Palestinians from Palestine in theory and in practice, yet they are still there.

THE FRIENDSHIP BETWEEN ISRAEL
AND APARTHEID SOUTH AFRICA

Over the years there was a good deal of warmth between the respective leaders of the South African apartheid regime and Israel. South Africa's Daniel Malan was the first prime minister to visit Jerusalem in 1953, but long before Israeli statehood was proclaimed, a personal friendship had thrived between Chaim Weizmann, who became Israel's first president, and Jan Smuts, South African prime minister and senior military leader for the British.[23] Weizmann often turned to Smuts in times of crisis – and 'both men took for granted the moral legitimacy of each other's respective position'.[24]

Israel eventually became a prominent supporter of the apartheid regime in South Africa, leading to a 1984 UN General Assembly Resolution specifically condemning 'the increasing collaboration by Israel with the racist regime of South Africa'.[25] While many countries supported apartheid, what is interesting in the case of Israel is the extent of the shared empathy. In the early 1960s, for example, Hendrik Verwoerd, the South African prime minister, shared his own view that 'the Jews took Israel from the Arabs after the Arabs had lived there for a thousand years. Israel, like South Africa, is an apartheid state.'[26]

In 1976, then South African Prime Minister John Vorster – a man who had been a Nazi sympathiser in World War II – was afforded a state banquet during a visit to Israel. At the official welcome, Israel's Yitzhak Rabin made a toast to 'the ideals shared by Israel and South Africa: the hopes for justice and peaceful coexistence.'[27] The following year, the 'Official Yearbook of the Republic of South Africa' noted that 'Israel and South Africa have one thing above all else in common: they are both situated in a predominantly hostile world inhabited by dark peoples.'[28]

IN CONCLUSION

Increasingly, Israelis, Palestinians, South Africans and international observers are pointing out the parallels between apartheid South Africa and Israel. Several prominent South Africans have expressed their solidarity with the Palestinians, denouncing what they see as a similar (or worse) structure of oppression to the apartheid regime many of them fought against.

In 2002, veteran anti-apartheid figure and human rights campaigner, Archbishop Desmond Tutu made headlines with his article 'Apartheid in the Holy Land'.[29] Describing himself as 'deeply distressed' after a trip to Palestine/Israel that had reminded him 'so much of what happened to us black people in South Africa', the Archbishop affirmed that 'Israel will never get true security and safety through oppressing another people'.

In 2007, the UN Human Rights Rapporteur John Dugard, South African legal professor and apartheid expert, said that 'Israel's laws and practices in the OPT certainly resemble aspects of apartheid', echoing other South African trade union leaders, politicians, church groups and academics.[30] Western media correspondents have also made the comparison.[31]

Even Israeli politicians and commentators are now talking about apartheid, or more specifically, the risk of Israel facing a similar civil rights struggle that eventually prevailed in South Africa.[32] Indeed, albeit from quite a different perspective on the matter, Israel's foreign ministry predicted in 2004 that if the 'conflict with the Palestinians is not resolved', Israel 'could turn into a pariah state, on a par with South Africa during the apartheid years'.[33]

It is important to realise, however, that to compare the situation in Palestine/Israel to apartheid South Africa is not to try and force a 'one size fits all' political analysis where there are clear differences, as well as similarities. Rather, any such comparison is useful in so far as it helps sheds light – in Israel's case – on a political system that is based on structural racism, separation and dominance.

Moreover, as the rest of this book explains, even leaving aside the specific comparison with South Africa, Israel's past and present policies towards the indigenous Palestinians fully meet the aforementioned definition of apartheid laid out in international law – and urgently need to be treated as such by the international community.

Part I: Israeli Independence, Palestinian Catastrophe

We must expel Arabs and take their places.[1]

Ben-Gurion in a letter to his son, 1937

'Ben-Gurion was right...Without the uprooting of the Palestinians, a Jewish state would not have arisen here.'[2]

Benny Morris, Israeli historian

In August 1897, in the Swiss city of Basle, a meeting took place that would have profound and disastrous consequences for the Palestinians – though they were not present at the event, or even mentioned by the participants. The First Zionist Congress, the brainchild of Zionism's chief architect Theodor Herzl, resulted in the creation of the Zionist Organisation (later the World Zionist Organisation) and the publication of the Basle Programme – a kind of early Zionist manifesto.

Just the year before, Herzl had published 'The Jewish State', in which he laid out his belief that the only solution to the anti-semitism of European societies was for the Jews to have their own country. Writing in his diary a few days afterwards, Herzl predicted what the real upshot would be of the Congress:

> At Basle I founded the Jewish State. If I said this aloud today, I would be answered by universal laughter. In five years perhaps, and certainly in fifty years, everyone will perceive this.[3]

Herzl's Zionism was a response to European anti-semitism and, while a radical development, built on the foundations of more spiritually and culturally focused Jewish settlers who had already gone to Palestine on a very small scale. At the time, many Jews, for different reasons, disagreed with Herzl's answer to the 'Jewish question'. Nevertheless, the Zionists got to work; sending new settlers, securing financial support and bending the ear of the imperial powers without whose cooperation, the early leaders knew, the Zionist project would be impossible to realise.

At the beginning of the twentieth century, the population of Palestine was around 4 per cent Jewish and 96 per cent Palestinian Arab (of which around 11 per cent were Christian and the rest Muslim).[4] Before the new waves of Zionist settlers, the Palestinian Jewish community was 'small but of long standing', and concentrated 'in the four cities of religious significance: Jerusalem, Safed, Tiberias and Hebron'.[5] As new Zionist immigrants arrived, with the help of outside donations, French experts were called upon to share their experience of French colonisation in North Africa.[6]

An early priority for the Zionists was to secure more land on which to establish a secure, expanded, Jewish community. In 1901, the Jewish National Fund (JNF) was founded, an organisation 'devoted exclusively to the acquisition of land in Palestine for Jewish settlement'.[7] The JNF was destined to play a significant role in the history of Zionism, particularly as the land it acquired, by definition, 'became inalienably Jewish, never to be sold to or worked by non-Jews'.[8]

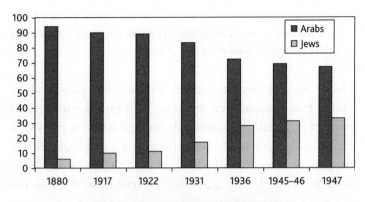

Chart 1   Palestine population, 1880–1947

Source: *Facts and Figures About the Palestinians*, Washington, DC:
The Center for policy analysis on Palestine, 1992, p. 7.

The land purchased by the JNF was often sold by rich, absentee land-owners from surrounding Arab countries. However, much of the land was worked by Palestinian tenant farmers, who were then forcibly removed after the JNF had bought the property. Thousands of peasant farmers and their families were made homeless and landless in such a manner.[9]

The Zionists knew early on that the support of an imperial power would be vital. Zionism emerged in the 'age of empire' and thus 'Herzl sought to secure a charter for Jewish colonization guaranteed by one or other imperial European power'. [10] Herzl's initial contact with the British led to discussions over different possible locations for colonisation, from an area in the Sinai Peninsula to a part of modern day Kenya.[11] Once agreed on Palestine, the Zionists recognised, in the words of future president Weizmann, it would be under Britain's 'wing' that the 'Zionist scheme' would be carried out.[12]

The majority of British policy-makers and ministers viewed political Zionism with favour for a variety of reasons. For an empire competing for influence in a key geopolitical region of the world, helping birth a natural ally would reap dividends. From the mid nineteenth century onwards, there was also a tradition of a more emotional and even religious support for the creation of a Jewish state in Palestine amongst Christians in positions of influence, including Lord Shaftesbury and Prime Minister Lloyd George.[13]

Britain's key role is most famously symbolised by the Balfour Declaration, sent in a letter in 1917 by then Foreign Secretary Arthur Balfour to Lord Rothschild. The Declaration announced that the British government viewed 'with favour the establishment in Palestine of a national home for the Jewish people' and moreover, promised to 'use their best endeavours to facilitate the achievement of this object'. At the time, Jews were less than 10 per cent of Palestine's population.[14]

In the end, the role of the imperial powers proved crucial. For all the differences between some in the British foreign policy establishment and members of the Zionist movement – as well as the open conflict between radical Zionist terror groups and British soldiers – it was under British rule that the Zionists were able to prepare for the conquest of Palestine. Ben-Gurion once joked, after visiting the Houses of Parliament in London, 'that he might as well have been at the Zionist Congress, the speakers had been so sympathetic to Zionism'.[15]

Differences between the Zionist leaders of various political stripes were essentially tactical. As Ben-Gurion explained, nobody argued about the 'indivisibility' of 'Eretz Israel' (the name usually used to refer to the total area of the Biblical 'Promised Land').[16] Rather, 'the debate was over which of two routes would lead quicker to the common goal'. In 1937, Weizmann told the British high commissioner that 'we shall expand in the whole country in the course of time ... this is only an arrangement for the next 25 to 30 years'.[17]

A LAND WITHOUT A PEOPLE ...

There is a fundamental difference in quality between Jew and native.[18]
Chaim Weizmann, Israel's first president

The Zionist leadership's view of the 'natives' was unavoidable – 'wanting to create a purely Jewish, or predominantly Jewish, state in an Arab Palestine' could only lead to the development 'of a racist state of mind'.[19] Moreover, Zionism was conceived as a Jewish response to a problem facing Jews; the Palestinian Arabs were a complete irrelevance.

In the early days, the native Palestinians were entirely ignored – airbrushed from their own land – or treated with racist condescension, portrayed as simple, backward folk who would benefit from Jewish colonisation. One more annoying obstacle to the realisation of Zionism, as Palestinian opposition increased, the 'natives' became increasingly portrayed as violent and dangerous. For the Zionists, Palestine was 'empty'; not literally, but in terms of people of equal worth to the incoming settlers.

The early Zionist leaders expressed an ideology very similar to that of other settler movements in other parts of the world, particularly with regards to the dismissal of the natives' past and present relationship to the land. Palestine was considered a 'desert' that the Zionists would 'irrigate' and 'till' until 'it again becomes the blooming garden it once was'.[20] The 'founding father' of political Zionism, Theodor Herzl, wrote in 1896 that in Palestine, a Jewish state would 'form a part of a wall of defense for Europe in Asia, an outpost of civilization against barbarism'.[21]

Many British officials shared the Zionist view of the indigenous Palestinians. In a conversation, the head of the Jewish Agency's colonisation department asked Weizmann about the Palestinian Arabs. Weizmann replied that 'the British told us that there are some hundred thousand negroes and for those there is no value'.[22]

Winston Churchill, meanwhile, explained his support for Jewish settlement in Palestine in explicitly racist terms. Comparing Zionist colonisation to what had happened to indigenous peoples in North America and Australia, Churchill could not 'admit that a wrong has been done to those people by the fact that a stronger race, a higher grade race, or, at any rate, a more worldly-wise race, to put it that way, has come in and taken their place'.[23]

The Zionist movement was passionately opposed to democratic principles being applied to Palestine, for obvious reasons. As first Israeli Prime Minister Ben-Gurion admitted in 1944, 'there is no example in history of a people saying we agree to renounce our country'.[24] At the beginning of British Mandate rule in Palestine, the Zionist Organization in London explained that the 'problem' with democracy is that it

> too commonly means majority rule without regard to diversities of types or stages of civilization or differences of quality ... if the crude arithmetical conception of democracy were to be applied now or at some early stage in the future to Palestinian conditions, the majority that would rule would be the Arab majority ...[25]

As late as 1947, the director of the US State Department Office of Near Eastern and African Affairs warned that the plans to create a Jewish state 'ignore such principles as self-determination and majority rule', an opinion shared by 'nearly every member of the Foreign Service or of the department who has worked to any appreciable extent on Near Eastern problems'.[26]

THE 'TRANSFER' CONSENSUS:

'Disappearing' the Arabs lay at the heart of the Zionist dream, and was also a necessary condition of its realization.[27]

Tom Segev, Israeli journalist and historian

If there are other inhabitants there, they must be transferred to some other place. We must take over the land.[28]

Menahem Ussishkin, chairman of JNF, member of the Jewish Agency, 1930

There was a logical outcome to the Zionist view of the indigenous Palestinians. As Israeli historian Benny Morris described it, 'from the start, the Zionists wished to make the area of Palestine a Jewish state'.[29] But 'unfortunately' the country already 'contained a native Arab population'. The 'obvious and most logical' solution was 'moving or transferring all or most of the Arabs out of its prospective territory'.[30]

How this ethnic cleansing was achieved is described later on, but for now, it is important to realise just how central the idea of 'transfer' (the preferred euphemism) was to Zionist thinking and strategising. The need to ethnically cleanse Palestine of its native Arabs was understood at all levels of the Zionist leadership, starting with Ben-Gurion himself. More than a decade before the State of Israel was born, the Zionist leader told the 20th Zionist Congress that 'the growing Jewish power in the country will increase our possibilities to carry out a large transfer'.[31]

Forcing out the Palestinians was only a problem for Ben-Gurion in terms of practicalities, as he did 'not see anything immoral' in 'compulsory transfer'.[32] By 1948, Ben-Gurion was 'projecting a message of transfer', and had created a consensus in favour of it.[33] A few months after becoming Prime Minister of the new state, Ben-Gurion said that 'the Arabs of the Land of Israel' had 'but one function left – to run away'.[34]

Ben-Gurion was not the only leader explicit about the need to ethnically cleanse Palestine. Joseph Weitz, JNF Director of Land and Forestry for 40 years, was passionate about the need for transfer. In a meeting of the so-called 'Committee for Population Transfer' in 1937, Weitz pointed out that:

> the transfer of Arab population from the area of the Jewish state does not serve only one aim – to diminish the Arab population. It also serves a second, no less important aim which is to evacuate land presently held and cultivated by the Arabs and thus to release it for the Jewish inhabitants.[35]

Weitz was a key influence on pre-state Zionist 'thinking and policy', 'well-placed to shape and influence decision-making regarding the Arab population on the national level and to oversee the implementation of policy on the local level'.[36] Others with powerful positions in the Zionist movement expressed their support for transfer, such as the director of the Jewish Agency (JA)'s immigration department, who told a JA Executive meeting in 1944 that the 'large minority' (the Palestinian Arabs) set to be inside Israel 'must be ejected'.[37]

That almost 'none of the Zionists disputed the desirability of forced transfer – or its morality' should not be a surprise: 'transfer was inevitable and inbuilt into Zionism – because it sought to transform a land which was 'Arab' into a 'Jewish' state'.[38] It explains the 'virtual pro-transfer consensus' in the JA Executive, and indeed, the support for transfer amongst the Zionist leadership's leading lights in the 1920s, 1930s and 1940s.[39]

In fact, the historical evidence that we *do* have regarding the Zionist desire for 'transfer' probably only represents a fragment of the total amount. Early on, Zionist leaders learned that 'under no circumstances should they talk as though the Zionist program required the expulsion of the Arabs' since 'this would cause the Jews to lose the world's sympathy'.[40] Thus while in public, 'discretion and circumspection' were necessary, 'in private, the Zionist leaders were more forthcoming'.[41]

Sometimes, there was more overt self-censorship. For example, the Jewish press coverage of the 20th Zionist

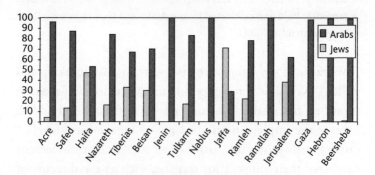

Chart 2   Palestine population by subdistrict in 1946

Source: Walid Khalidi, *Before Their Diaspora*, Washington, DC: Institute for Palestine Studies, 1984, p. 239.

Congress 'failed to mention that Ben-Gurion, or anyone else, had come out strongly in favour of transfer', and when the Zionist Organization published the official text of the addresses given at the Congress, 'controversial' sections were omitted.[42] Those taking minutes in meetings of Zionist organisations could be asked to 'take a break' 'and thus to exclude from the record discussion on such matters' such as 'transfer'.[43]

THE CALM BEFORE THE STORM

By the time that Britain had decided to get out of Palestine and hand the problem over to the United Nations, the Zionists were ready for the revolutionary moment they knew was necessary to create a Jewish state in Palestine. Effective Zionist lobbying, particularly in the USA, combined with an ineffective strategy from the Arabs, meant that when it came to the vote, 33 nations voted in favour of partition, 10 abstained and 13 rejected the plan.[44]

Partition was not the reasonable compromise it can sound like. The Palestinian Arabs were more than two thirds of the population of Palestine, and were a majority in all but one of the 16 sub-districts (Chart 2).[45] Jews owned around 20 per cent of the cultivable land, and just over 6 per cent of the total land of Palestine.[46]

Despite the fact that Jews were a clear minority in terms of both population and land ownership, the Partition Plan handed over 55.5 per cent of Palestine to the proposed Jewish state (Israel would later increase that by strength of arms to 78 per cent). The Palestinian Arabs would make up almost half the population of the new Jewish state, territory even set to include the Negev which was 1 per cent Jewish.[47] The Jewish state would include prime agricultural land and '40 percent of Palestinian industry and the major sources of the country's electrical supply'.[48]

Given that the indigenous Palestinians, without their consultation, were set to lose more than half their country to a settler population who explicitly wished to alienate the land from the Arabs forever, it has taken quite a feat of propaganda to represent the Palestinian rejection of 'Partition' as inflexible and irrational.

At the time, there were a few dissenting voices, Jews who opposed the violent conquest of Palestine and instead favoured sharing the land with the Palestinian Arabs.[49] But by the time of the unilateral declaration of Israeli statehood in May 1948, the vast majority of the Zionist leadership was prepared for the forced 'transfer' they knew was necessary for the old propaganda slogan of a 'land without a people' to become a darkly self-fulfilling prophecy.

Far from being weak and outnumbered, a British military intelligence assessment in 1947 had 'estimated that an embryonic Jewish state would defeat the Palestinian Arabs' even if they were secretly helped by neighbouring Arab states.[50] Throughout the war, in fact, Jewish forces 'significantly outnumbered all the Arab forces' sometimes by nearly two to one.[51]

THE NAKBA (CATASTROPHE)

The dismantling of Palestinian society, the destruction of Palestinian towns and villages, and the expulsion of 700,000 Palestinians ... was a deliberate and planned operation intended to 'cleanse' (the term used in the declassified documents) those parts of Palestine assigned to the Jews as a necessary pre-condition for the emergence of a Jewish state.[52]

Henry Siegman, *The New York Review of Books*

Another prominent left-winger stated: 'I don't have any problem with the fact that we threw them out, and we don't want them back, because we want a Jewish state.'[53]

Cited by Meron Benvenisti, in *Sacred Landscape*

The term 'ethnic cleansing' is a relatively recent addition to the English language, originating from conflict in the Balkans in the latter part of the twentieth century. Using the expression can immediately conjure up televised images of faraway wars and horrific brutality; but an exact definition is surprisingly hard to come by.

In 1993, *Foreign Affairs* journal carried an article on the subject, where the author admitted the difficulty in pinning down a definition.[54] Nevertheless, he concluded that 'at the most general level', ethnic cleansing is 'the expulsion of an "undesirable" population from a given territory due to religious or ethnic discrimination, political, strategic or ideological considerations, or a combination of these'.

The following year, the *European Journal of International Law* published a piece by Drazen Petrovic about identifying a 'methodology' of ethnic cleansing.[55] Petrovic noted that it is probable the term had its origin 'in military vocabulary', where 'cleaning' a territory is used 'in the final phase of combat in order to take total control of the conquered territory'. 'Ethnic' is added because 'the "enemies" are considered to be the other ethnic communities'.

On the local level, ethnic cleansing policies include 'the creation of fear, humiliation and terror for the "other" community' and 'provoking the community to flee', with the overall aim being 'the extermination of certain groups of people from a particular territory, including the elimination of all physical traces of their presence'.

Even more revealingly for our focus on Palestine in 1948, Petrovic also differentiates between the short- and long-term goals of ethnic cleansing policies. In the short term, the goal 'could be effective control over territory for military or strategic reasons', but long term, the objective is 'the creation of living conditions that would make the return of the displaced community impossible'.

The Palestinian Catastrophe ticks all of the boxes. The Zionist leadership understood it (we have already read about their pre-war strategising on the matter), as did the soldiers on the ground. In the Jewish military plans, Palestinian villages became 'enemy bases', their inhabitants 'dehumanised in order to turn them into "legitimate targets" of destruction and expulsion'.[56]

Some Zionist propagandists, unable to sustain any longer the long-standing lie that the Palestinians were told to leave by the Arab armies or simply left of their own volition, now try and suggest that the absence of documents signed by the Zionist leadership ordering blanket expulsions is somehow proof the ethnic cleansing never occurred.

In reality, once you dig beneath the surface, there is no shortage of evidence of orders from superiors to units on the ground. Moreover, it is now well known that Ben-Gurion 'usually resorted to a nod and a wink' rather than 'explicit orders', keenly and 'constantly aware of how history would judge his deeds'.[57] Israel's Prime Minister did, however, keep track in his diary of the so-called 'occupied and evicted villages'.[58]

The word 'cleansing' in Hebrew, *tihur*, was on 'every order that the High Command passed down to the units on the ground', while individual villages were either ordered to be 'cleansed' or 'destroyed'.[59] Haganah (the official pre-state Jewish armed forces) orders in April 1948 were 'explicitly calling for the "liquidation" [*hisul*] of villages'.[60] A standard operational order of May 1948 instructed the army company concerned:

> to expel the enemy from the villages ... to clean the front line ...To conquer the villages, to cleanse them of inhabitants (women and children should [also] be expelled), to take several prisoners ... [and] to burn the greatest possible number of houses.[61]

An important role in the ethnic cleansing of Palestine was played by the so-called 'Plan Dalet', adopted by the Haganah military leaders in March 1948. The aim of the plan was 'to clear the interior of the country of hostile and potentially

Photograph 1   Palestinians leaving their homeland after the Arab-Israeli war of 1948 (UNRWA photo, 1948).

hostile Arab elements', and thus 'permitted and justified the forcible expulsion of Arab civilians'.[62] In May, Ben-Gurion wrote a letter to the Haganah brigade commanders to remind them that 'the cleansing of Palestine remained the prime objective of Plan Dalet'.[63] By the end of March, the head of the Haganah had already appointed a 'Committee for Arab Property' charged with managing the increasing number of empty Palestinian villages and homes.[64]

Khaled Diab

'I remember everything. On the night of October 27, 1948, it became clear that the village would soon fall to the Israeli army. The people fled in fear of a massacre similar to the several others that happened in villages like Deir Yassin, where more than 100 men, women and children were murdered in cold blood by Israeli forces. All those who could walk across the Galilee Mountains to Lebanon did. But due to the birth of my sister one month before, my parents couldn't walk the distance to Lebanon, so they stayed. After more than 20 hours of walking in fear we arrived in Lebanon. We slept under trees with a blanket that was given to us. We thought we would be in Syria for a few weeks, only until we were allowed to return home.'

Source: Institute for Middle East Understanding, 'Untold stories: Khaled Diab', 9 April 2008, http://imeu.net/news/article008407.shtml.

MASSACRES AND EXPULSIONS

In another meeting Ben-Gurion stated, 'We decided to clean out Ramle.'[65]

Tom Segev

Creating terror and panic amongst civilians through atrocities – as well as direct, forced expulsions – are an integral part of an ethnic cleansing campaign. Estimates for the number of massacres carried out in 1948 vary – 24 is one suggestion, 33 another.[66] Some atrocities, when dozens of Palestinians were executed at a time, are easier to agree on as constituting a 'massacre'. But there were also many cases of random killings: 'two old men are spotted walking in a field – they are shot. A woman is found in an abandoned village – she is shot.'[67]

Massacres were significant because of the way in which they created a general sense of panic amongst neighbouring villages and towns, and a subsequent increase in Palestinians who fled their homes in fear (unbeknown to them at the time, never to return). Deir Yassin remains one of the most notorious massacres, where between 100 and 120 villagers were murdered, including families shot down 'as they left their homes and fled down alleyways'.[68]

Deir Yassin was far from being an isolated case of the deliberate murder of civilians. In the village of Khisas, for example, in December 1947, Jewish forces 'randomly started blowing up houses at the dead of night while occupants were still fast asleep', an attack that killed 15 villagers.[69] After the incident received unwelcome international attention, Ben-Gurion publicly apologised – only a few months later to include the assault 'in a list of successful operations'.

Across the country, Palestinians were terrorised into leaving. In Mejd al-Kroom, twelve men were randomly selected and shot dead in front of the others, while in Safsaf, 70 Palestinians were murdered in front of the villagers who had not already run for their lives.[70] In Dawayima in October 1948, 'villagers were gunned down inside houses, in the alleyways and on the surrounding slopes as they fled' (80–100 died).[71]

The massacres were often a prelude to the emptying of individual villages. While many Palestinians left their homes through fear of the advancing Zionist forces, some were forcibly driven from their communities by soldiers. A notorious case in point was the ethnic cleansing of Ramla and Lydda in the summer of 1948, two neighbouring Palestinian cities actually outside the intended borders of the Jewish state.[72]

In Lydda, the military assault ended with a handful of Israeli soldiers and hundreds of Palestinians dead. Shortly after conquering both towns, Israeli soldiers began expelling the population. Yitzhak Rabin, a commander at the time, had asked Ben-Gurion what should be done about the inhabitants, to which the prime minister responded dismissively, 'Expel them.'[73]

In Ramla, the Israeli soldiers banged on the doors of houses with 'the butts of their guns' shouting through bullhorns 'go to Ramallah!'[74] Altogether, an estimated 50,000 Palestinians were forced to march to the West Bank, with some of the refugees dying on the road 'from exhaustion, dehydration and disease'.[75] In Lydda, which became the Israeli town of Lod, around 98 per cent of the Palestinian population were expelled.[76]

Other communities experienced a similar fate, with incidents of emptied villages mined to prevent Palestinians returning, shots being fired over fleeing civilians to 'encourage' their flight, and columns of refugees targeted with mortar fire and makeshift bombs dropped by aircraft – all 'to speed them on their way'.[77]

Despite the mass of available evidence from eyewitnesses, survivors, perpetrators and historians, Zionist apologists have tried to confuse the issue about why the Palestinian refugees left their homes. One oft-repeated lie is that the refugees were simply responding to orders by advancing Arab forces, a propaganda claim tied up with the idea that the nascent Israeli state was fighting a desperate war of self-defence.

In fact, the ethnic cleansing of Palestine began *before* Israel unilaterally declared independence, and before the Arab states had (half-heartedly) joined the battle. An estimated half of the eventual total of dispossessed Palestinians had been 'cleansed' before the 'Arab-Israeli' war even began.[78]

In a period of less than seven weeks leading up to Israel's creation and the Arab-Israeli war, 200 Palestinian villages 'were occupied and their inhabitants expelled'.[79] From 15 May to the time of the first truce in June, a further 90 villages were 'wiped out'. Even before that, starting in December 1947, the evacuation of Palestinians from their towns and villages was principally due to Jewish 'attacks or fear of impending attack'.[80] It was a pattern that would continue through April–June of 1948, when every 'exodus occurred during or in the immediate wake of military assault'.[81]

Historian and Middle East specialist, Charles D. Smith affirms that during the war with the Arab states, 'the Israelis embarked on a deliberate policy of ousting Arabs from the territories they took over'.[82] Israeli historian Ilan Pappe observes that 'not allowing people to return to their homes after a short stay abroad is as much expulsion as any other act directed against the local people with the aim of deportation'.[83] Historian Benny Morris, likewise, makes it clear where responsibility lies:

Above all, let me reiterate, the refugee problem was caused by attacks by Jewish forces on Arab villages and towns and by the inhabitants' fear of such attacks, compounded by expulsions, atrocities, and rumours of atrocities – and by the crucial Israeli Cabinet decision in June 1948 to bar a refugee return.[84]

SHOOTING THE HARVESTERS

Even as Israel was concluding armistice agreements with the Arab states, there were acts of ethnic cleansing. In January 1949, almost 1,000 Palestinians were expelled, while others were 'transferred' to other villages inside the new Jewish state.[85] A couple of months later, a further few hundred Palestinians were expelled from two villages, usually forcibly taken to the West Bank in trucks.[86] In June, up to 1,500 Palestinian refugees were violently 'pushed across the border' in one night, while in November, an estimated 1,500–2,500 Bedouin were again 'pushed' over the border.[87]

A striking example of these 'belated' expulsions was the experience of the Palestinian city of Majdal. The majority of the town's population had fled in fear of the advancing

---

Nimr Khatib

'So the people of Mujaydil were forced to flee...While we were escaping there was shooting at us. Of those who escaped through the main road to Nazareth ... four or five young men were killed and wounded... Some other people stayed in their hideaway... a great number of them were killed in the olive groves...The old people and children who couldn't run away and escape ... hid in the Latin monastery till the next day, [when] the army vehicles arrived and took them and let them down on the edge of Nazareth. We heard that the old men and women who could not leave the houses and didn't get to Nazareth – after a period of time their families crept into al-Mujaydil and found them dead, killed in the houses. And from that time they sealed off al-Mujaydil and not one of the people was allowed to enter...'

Source: Nakba Oral Histories, as told to Isabelle Humphries, *Washington Report on Middle East Affairs*, May–June 2008, pp.28–9, http://www.wrmea.com/archives/May-June_2008/0805028.html.

Jewish forces, but some had remained. In November 1948, around 500 were expelled from Majdal to the Gaza Strip.[88] During 1949, hundreds of Palestinians managed to return to the town, but meanwhile, the Israeli government was busy settling new Jewish families there.[89]

These remaining Palestinians were put under military government, 'concentrated and sealed off with barbed wire and IDF guards in a small, built-up area commonly known as the "ghetto"'. The formal transfer of the town's 'undesirable' population was completed between June and October of 1950, so that eventually, there was an 'Arab-free Majdal'.[90] This became the Israeli port city of Ashkelon.

The problem faced by Israeli authorities in Majdal, of a returning Palestinian population, was a challenge faced in other parts of the country. These returning refugees were dubbed 'infiltrators'. Having gone to such trouble to 'cleanse' Palestine of its unwanted natives, the Israeli leadership was not prepared to tolerate even a piecemeal return; Prime Minister Ben-Gurion once said 'he viewed the infiltration problem "through the barrel of a gun"'.[91]

Typically, there was the 'security' excuse, justified by the incidents of persons crossing the border into Israel in order to carry out armed attacks. However, between 1949 and 1956, at least 90 per cent of all 'infiltrators' were motivated by social or economic concerns: they wanted to return home, search for relatives, harvest their crops and recover lost possessions.[92]

Israeli armed forces were brutal in their response to the returning refugees. Women and children, who had only crossed the frontier by a matter of a few hundred yards to gather crops, were murdered. Those 'wounded by patrols or ambushes were often killed off on the spot'.[93] The estimates for the total number of 'infiltrators' killed up to 1956 range between 2,700 and 5,000; the 'great majority of them unarmed'.[94]

WHEN THE DUST CLEARED

It would be an offence against the principles of elemental justice if these innocent victims of the conflict were denied the right to return to their homes while Jewish immigrants flow into Palestine and indeed, at least offer the threat of permanent replacement of the Arab refugees.[95]

Count Folke Bernadotte, United Nations Palestine mediator, assassinated in Jerusalem the day after his report was published in September 1948

The policy was to prevent a refugee return at all costs... In this sense, it may fairly be said that all 700,000 or so who ended up as refugees were compulsorily displaced or 'expelled'.[96]

Benny Morris, Israeli historian

Physically preventing the return of refugees, however, was just one small part of a far bigger plan to make the ethnic cleansing a permanent fact and secure Palestinian land for the Jewish state. In June 1948, JNF director Josef Weitz had a meeting with Prime Minister Ben-Gurion in order to share the recommendations of the Transfer Committee. According to Weitz, Ben-Gurion 'agreed to the whole line'.[97]

There were five specific proposals: destroy villages as much as possible, prevent Palestinians cultivating their land, settle Jews in some of the villages and towns, enact tailor-made legislation and employ propaganda against a return. The legislation carried out will be examined in more detail in Part II, as Israel first categorised the refugees' land as 'absentee property' before transferring it all to the state Development Authority.[98]

Initially, however, the most fervent concentration of activity was focused on destroying the emptied villages, parcelling out their land to neighbouring Jewish settlements and, in some cases, directly repopulating Palestinian towns with Jews. The number of Palestinian villages and towns ethnically cleansed range from over 350 to more than 500 (often depending on what is classified as a recognised community) (Map 2).[99]

While the exact numbers differ, the overall scale of the Zionist conquest is clear. Around 87 per cent of the Palestinians who had lived in what was now Israel had been removed, while the majority of the Negev's Bedouin population, numbering around 65,000 in the 1922 census, 'were expelled in successive waves after 1948'.[100] An estimated four in every five Palestinian towns and villages inside Israel were either totally destroyed, or immediately settled by Jews.[101]

Benny Morris records how the number of Jewish settlements in Palestine increased by almost 50 per cent between 1947 and 1949, with most built on Palestinian land.[102] Other estimates are that 95 per cent of new Jewish settlements established between 1948 and 1953 were on absentee Palestinian property.[103] Former Israeli deputy mayor of Jerusalem, Meron Benvenisti, has written of how, by mid 1949, 'two-thirds of all land sown with grain in Israel was abandoned Arab land'.[104]

In some cases, Palestinian towns emptied by atrocities and expulsions were more or less immediately resettled by the Israeli government with Jews. Ramle and Lydda, whose Palestinian population had been forced to trek eastwards, had a combined population of over 16,000 Jewish settlers by March 1950.[105] In 1949, Jewish immigrants were even settled in Deir Yassin. The dedication ceremony for the new settlement was attended by 'several Cabinet ministers, the two chief rabbis and Jerusalem's mayor'.[106]

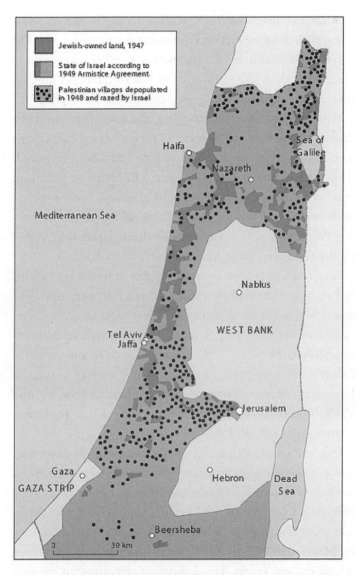

Legend:
- Jewish-owned land, 1947
- State of Israel according to 1949 Armistice Agreement
- Palestinian villages depopulated in 1948 and razed by Israel

Haifa

Sea of Galilee

Nazareth

Mediterranean Sea

Nablus

Tel Aviv
Jaffa

WEST BANK

Jerusalem

Gaza

Hebron

Dead Sea

GAZA STRIP

Beersheba

0   30 km

Map 2   Palestinian villages depopulated in 1948 and razed by Israel

Source: Adapted from Palestinian Academic Society
for the Study of International Affairs (PASSIA).

An important part of Israel's effort to 'disappear' Palestine was changing the names on the map. Ben-Gurion appointed a Negev Names Committee, saying that Israel was 'obliged' for 'reasons of state' to remove Arabic names.[107] Between May 1948 and March 1951, the Jewish National Fund's 'Naming Committee' 'assigned 200 new names'.[108]

Photograph 2   Palestinian refugees in Jordan, in the aftermath of the 1967 war (UNRWA photo by G. Nehmeh, 1968).

POSTSCRIPT: THE SECOND 'NAKBA' OF 1967

No factual and necessarily brief account can, however, portray the overwhelming sense of bewilderment and shock felt by the inhabitants of the areas affected by the hostilities as the cataclysm swept over them.[109]

UNRWA General-Commissioner,
UN General Assembly, June 1967

While the 1948 Nakba condemned hundreds of thousands of Palestinians to enforced exile and dispossession, it is often forgotten that during the 1967 Six Day War, Israel was able to expel many more Palestinians. Around 300,000 Palestinians fled or were expelled from the Gaza Strip and West Bank, the vast majority from the latter territory.[110] Like the Nakba, many of these refugees (some of whom had already been expelled in 1948) had been 'forcibly evicted from their homes', their villages bulldozed to ensure that they would not be able to return'.[111]

In 1967, the conditions did not exist for executing a repeat of the mass exodus on the scale of, or greater than 1948; in particular, there was far more international scrutiny. Israeli forces therefore resorted to a more psychological campaign of fear. The UN's on the ground investigator noted 'persistent reports of acts of intimidation', including the use of loudspeakers on cars recommending the population go to Jordan.[112]

Others have described how 'Israeli buses and trucks were made available to tens of thousands of frightened Palestinians who were warned to vacate their homes and flee or remain to find they had no home'.[113] At least half of those who left the West Bank were already UN registered refugees, while in Jericho, 90 per cent of the population fled their homes.[114] Ultimately, of the thousands who fled the West Bank, less than 8 per cent were allowed by Israel to return.

Apart from the general attempt at 'encouraging' population flight, there were also several incidents of more direct ethnic cleansing. In Jerusalem's Old City, just days after its conquest, Israel targeted the eight centuries-old Moroccan Quarter, ordering out hundreds of Palestinian families and demolishing all the homes.[115] The area then became the spacious plaza that exists until today in front of the Wailing Wall.

Meanwhile, in the Latroun area of the West Bank, close to the border with Israel proper, three villages were depopulated and destroyed. The Palestinian residents:

> were first told to leave their homes and gather in an open area outside the villages. At around nine in the morning, they were instructed over loudspeakers to march toward Ramallah. There were some eight thousand of them.[116]

An Israeli observer described how 'men and women, children and old people, had been forced to walk, in the stifling heat of over 30 degrees Centigrade, towards Ramallah, a distance of 30 km'.[117] The army then wasted no time, 'immediately' beginning to destroy the homes. In their place, Israel later built the recreational 'Canada Park', administered by the Jewish National Fund.[118]

The village of Beit Awa also met a similar fate. At 5.30 am on 11 June, the 2,500 inhabitants were ordered out of their homes by Israeli forces, who told them 'to take two loaves of bread and to go to the hills surrounding the village'.[119] Two hours later, the troops started to demolish the houses 'with dynamite and bulldozers'. Three hundred and sixty homes were destroyed before a fraction of the original population was permitted to return.[120]

Qalqilya, a substantial West Bank city (now penned in behind Israel's Separation Wall), was fortunate to survive the 1967 occupation at all. As it was, 850 of the city's 2,000 dwellings were destroyed by the Israeli army, 98 per cent of them after the actual fighting had finished.[121] One returning resident described how 'the streets were devastated and there were no features to identify the city as ours'.[122]

Perhaps the biggest localised population movement was in the Jordan Valley, on the eve of war home to three large refugee camps clustered near Jericho. One Israeli who visited the camps soon after the war described them as 'ghost towns'.[123] Only a few of the camps' inhabitants were allowed back by Israel; the Jordan Valley's population fell by 88 per cent. Israel's first settlements in the OPT were in the Jordan Valley.[124]

Photograph 3   Some of the tens of thousands of Palestinian refugees who fled the West Bank for Jordan in 1967 (UNRWA photo by G. Nehmeh).

ISRAELI INDEPENDENCE, PALESTINIAN CATASTROPHE: THE MAKING OF APARTHEID

Over the course of a generation, Palestine disappeared from the map. By 1970, just over seventy years since the Basle congress launched Herzl's dream of a Jewish state, Palestinian society had been shattered:

- Around half of all Palestinians were living outside of Palestine as dispossessed, denationalised refugees, prevented from returning home.
- One in seven Palestinians were living as second-class citizens in a state that defined itself as the homeland of the Jews.
- One in three Palestinians were living under military rule, increasingly subject to a regime of apartheid separation designed to facilitate the colonisation of the OPT by Israeli settlers. (Over half of the OPT population were themselves refugees from 1948.)

For political Zionism to come to fruition – for a Jewish state to be created in Palestine – it was necessary to carry out as large a scale as possible ethnic cleansing of the country's

Photograph 4 Dheisheh refugee camp, West Bank (Andy Sims, http//www.andysimsphotography.com).

unwanted Arab natives. But even in 1948, and especially in 1967, Israel was unable to fully 'cleanse' the land of the Palestinians. As a result, Israel's fallback position was to implement an apartheid regime of exclusion and discrimination. Where the dispossession had been most effective – inside Israel's pre-1967 borders – apartheid could be less explicit. But in the OPT, home to a vast majority of Palestinians, Israeli apartheid had to be overt and iron-fisted. In Part II, we will examine conditions for Palestinians living in both Israel and the OPT.

Part II: Israeli Apartheid

In 'Introducing Israeli Apartheid' we looked at a definition of apartheid under international law, and noted some of the useful comparisons with apartheid South Africa. In Part I, we saw how the Zionist settlement in Palestine developed, how the key figures directing the project for Jewish statehood were clear in their intention to expel the indigenous Palestinian Arabs, and how this dream became reality with the Palestinian Catastrophe in 1948.

Part II is concerned with describing just how Israeli apartheid has been maintained for the last 60 years; legally, practically, and what it has meant for the day to day lives of Palestinians inside Israel and the OPT. The first section deals with the way in which Israel has been able to regulate and legalise its system of apartheid, with a focus on the Palestinians inside the Jewish state. The second section examines the nature of Israel's occupation of the West Bank, Gaza Strip and East Jerusalem since 1967, a story of land theft, colonisation and ethnic separation.

ISRAEL: A STATE FOR *SOME* OF ITS CITIZENS

As a Zionist State, the State of Israel, contrary to other states, must regard itself as the State of a people the majority of which is not concentrated within its borders.[1]

One of the defences offered by apologists for Israel in the West is that Israel is unfairly 'singled out' amongst the countries of the world for condemnation. In fact, Israel is indeed a 'unique' case, but not in the way the propagandists like to acknowledge. Israel is not a state of all its citizens, like for example Britain, the USA or France, but rather a state for *some* of its citizens: Jews. Moreover, it is not just the state of its Jewish citizens: it identifies itself as the state of *all* the Jews worldwide, no matter where they live.[2]

Israel is in many respects admirably democratic, in terms of the electoral process and accountability, a robust legal system, as well as freedom of the press. Yet there is a fundamental contradiction at its core. As former Prime Minister Shamir put it, 'the Jewish state cannot exist without a special ideological content. We cannot exist for long like any other state whose main interest is to insure the welfare of its citizens.'[3]

This contradiction of a 'Jewish and democratic' state is highlighted by the distinction within Israeli law between citizenship and nationality.[4] All Israeli citizens (*ezrahut* in Hebrew) have equal rights in theory. But only its Jewish citizens are nationals (*le'um*) – because the whole purpose of political Zionism is a state for the Jewish nation. So, in fact, there is no such thing as 'Israeli' nationality in Israeli law, a distinction concealed by the fact that in Western democracies, 'citizenship' and 'nationality' are most commonly used inter-changeably.

This facet of Israeli law has been highlighted in the courts, when individuals have sought to challenge the status quo. In 1970, Israel's Supreme Court supported a district court judge's denial of the existence of an 'Israeli' nationality.[5] The district judge explained his decision by declaring that there 'is no Israeli nation that exists separately from a Jewish nation'.

More recently, a group of Israelis tried to again bring the issue to the court's attention (unsuccessfully, at the time of writing). One of the petitioners, Professor Uzzi Ornan, explained the inherent 'anti-democratic' nature of the citizenship/nationality distinction in Israel:

> Most countries have citizens who categorize themselves not only according to their country of origin, but by ethnic, religious or cultural affiliation as well; however, all are considered to be of the same nationality...Imagine the uproar amongst the Jewish communities in the US or France, if the authorities tried to list 'Jewish' or 'Christian' in any official document.[6]

A 'Jewish democracy', as Israel describes itself, is thus a contradiction in terms, and it is clear which part of the equation has precedence when it really matters. In 1985, with Shimon Peres as Prime Minister, an amendment was passed to a Basic Law (one of nine that are the closest thing Israel has to a written constitution) prohibiting participation in elections to the Knesset for candidates who 'expressly or by implication' oppose 'the existence of the State of Israel as the state of the Jewish people'.[7]

In the last few years Palestinians inside Israel have published serious, in-depth studies into the inherent discrimination of a Jewish state (also see Part III). The reaction was instructive: *The Jerusalem Post*'s editorial saw the call for a 'democratic, bilingual and multicultural' state as 'enticing and deceptive'.[8] A distinguished diplomat and academic condemned one constitutional draft as a plan 'for Israel's annihilation as a Jewish state' coated 'in the outward trappings of human rights and justice'.

What could be so threatening about a constitution based on human rights and justice?[9] Adalah, 'the legal centre Arab

Minority Rights in Israel', who authored one of the recent studies, noted that 'the reaction of the Israeli establishment ... has been one of hysteria', characteristic of colonial regimes, which viewed any challenge to their constitutional structure, based on repression, as a strategic threat:

> Such was the reaction of the Apartheid regime in the 1950s when the African National Congress proposed the Freedom Charter, in which it demanded the transformation of South Africa into a state of all its citizens ...[10]

INCLUSION AND EXCLUSION

> One certain truth is that there is no Zionist settlement and there is no Jewish State without displacing Arabs and without confiscating lands and fencing them off.[11]
> Yeshayahu Ben-Porat, *Yediot Aharonot* newspaper, 14 July 1972

Veteran Israeli activist Dr Uri Davis wrote in his seminal book *Apartheid Israel* how in 1950, 'the Israeli Knesset passed two defining laws': the Absentee Property Law, 'defining the boundaries of exclusion', and the Law of Return, 'defining the boundaries of inclusion'.[12]

The Law of Return has been described, in the absence of an Israeli constitution, as one of the state's 'most fundamental documents', defining 'the nation's raison d'etre' – namely, to be the national home for all Jewish people the world over.[13] In the words of Ben-Gurion, the Law has 'nothing to do with immigration laws' found in other countries.[14] The significance of the Law of Return is that since its passing:

Jews have been entitled to simply show up and declare themselves to be Israeli citizens... Essentially, all Jews everywhere are Israeli citizens by right.[15]

At the same time as it offered automatic entry to Jews the world over, the State of Israel took a significant step toward consolidating in law the dispossession that had been previously effected at the barrel of a gun. Around six months after Israeli independence had been declared, a Custodian of Absentee Property was appointed and given 'absolute powers' over the lands and properties belonging to the Palestinian refugees.[16]

The Absentee Property Law of 1950 declared land to be 'abandoned' if the owner or owners were absent for even just one day from November 1947. Naturally, this included all the Palestinians pushed over the borders of the new Jewish state. The singular purpose behind this definition of 'absentee property' was 'to justify the taking of Arab lands and buildings for the sake of consolidating Israel's hold on the bulk of the land area'.[17]

The Israeli government sent inspectors out to Palestinian communities throughout the 1950s and 1960s 'to claim the land of those who could be defined as absentees on behalf of the Custodian'.[18] In 1953, the Knesset passed the Land Acquisition (Validations of Acts and Compensation) Law which confirmed the government's title to the land previously classified as 'absentee'.[19]

While it was the Absentee Property Law and subsequent legislation which proved to be the primary means by which Israel confiscated Palestinian land, there are many other examples of laws being used to transfer property into Jewish possession. Crucial to the way in which Israel consolidated

its apartheid regime in the early years of statehood was
the military rule placed over the remaining Palestinians
until 1966.

The 'Defense (Emergency) Regulations' law meant that
around 85 per cent of the Palestinians inside Israel lived under
full martial law.[20] The military government was responsible
for curfews, dividing the Galilee into 58 administrative
sections, and implementing a 'permit' system for travel
between them. The Regulations were also used to confiscate
Palestinian land.

All in all, since 1948, Israel has passed 30 statutes
that 'expropriated and transferred land from Palestinian
citizens to state (Jewish) ownership'.[21] While most large-
scale dispossession was carried out in the early years of the
Israeli state, even in the 1990s, legislation like the 'Public
Purposes Ordinance' was being used to confiscate hundreds
of thousands of dunams of private Palestinian land.[22]

By the mid 1970s, the average Palestinian community
had lost around 65–75 per cent of its land.[23] Palestinian
loss was Jewish gain: 350 of the 370 new Jewish settlements
established between 1948 and 1953 were on Palestinian
land.[24] Almost 200,000 Jews moved into empty Arab towns
and villages, while in so-called 'mixed cities', Palestinians
were concentrated in specified 'Arab quarters'.[25]

The legal infrastructure of Israeli apartheid is more
sophisticated and complicated than that of apartheid South
Africa, and necessarily so. For 'had discrimination against
Palestinians been written into Israeli law as specifically as discrimination against Blacks is written into South African law,
outside support would surely be jeopardized'.[26] The key then
is to understand the role played by the so-called 'National

Institutions' and in particular the legal mechanisms related to land ownership in Israel.

Hussein Mubaraki

'I am from al-Nahr, in the district of Akka, a village of 420 people. The village was 6,000 dunams (1,500 acres), including a river. It was a village rich in water, with fertile lands. Every day we had a wagon full of oranges, lemons and other produce which would go out to the cities, to Akka and Haifa...

[In 1948] we fled to Abu Snaan village ... no, first we went to Tarshiha – then they hit Tarshiha with planes – and we came here... Just two or three families from our village found shelter here, not more... the rest are in Lebanon...

Military rule was like this: they made the military rule so that when we came from al-Nahr to here we couldn't go [back] there – it was a military zone... So that people couldn't go. If people went they would put them in prison. If you entered the military zone ... that's what happened. In order to take the land...'

Source: Nakba Oral Histories, as told to Isabelle Humphries, *Washington Report on Middle East Affairs*, May–June 2008, pp.28–9, http://www.wrmea. com/archives/May-June_2008/0805028.html.

VEILING APARTHEID

Dr Uri Davis relates Israel's dilemma: on the one hand, 'the new state was politically and legally committed to the values of the Universal Declaration of Human Rights, the Charter of the United Nations Organization, and the standards of international law'.[27] Yet on the other hand, the 'driving force underpinning the efforts of political Zionism' was definitely not 'liberal democratic'.

While the 'key distinction' in Israeli apartheid is between 'Jew' and 'non-Jew', this is rarely explicitly stated in the text of Knesset legislation.[28] Instead, there is a 'two-tier structure' which 'has preserved the veil of ambiguity over Israeli apartheid legislation for over half a century'. The first tier is the Zionist institutions – the Jewish National Fund (JNF), World Zionist Organization (WZO) and Jewish Agency (JA) – that exist for the benefit of Jews.

The second tier is the way in which these institutions are 'incorporated into the body of the laws of the State of Israel', and in particular, 'the body of strategic legislation governing land tenure'.[29] This way, an organisation like the JNF, whose own constitution outlines the group's purpose as 'settling Jews' on the land, is assigned responsibilities and authority normally reserved for the government.

The benefits of this two-tier system are clear, as Ben-Gurion himself acknowledged. Israel's first Prime Minister described how the Zionist Organization 'is able to achieve what is beyond the power and competence of the State' which is precisely 'the advantage of the Zionist Organization over the State'.[30]

The JNF, as has already been described in Part I, was the organisation that took charge of land purchasing in the early days of Zionist colonisation. But with the creation of the State of Israel, the JNF did not go out of business. By October 1950, the government sale of land to the JNF had tripled its holdings, including around 40 per cent of Palestinian 'abandoned' land.[31]

The JNF was assigned three crucial roles in the Israeli apartheid infrastructure: firstly, it became a significant landholder in its own right; secondly, it was 'assigned specific tasks in the state that were by their nature governmental functions'; and thirdly, the JNF was given 'shared responsibility with the state for managing Israel Lands, now over 93 per cent of all land in Israel'.[32]

The body that was created to oversee the management of some 93 per cent of Israeli land is the Israel Lands Administration (ILA). Policy is set by the Israel Land Council, whose 22 members are made up of representatives of government ministers (twelve) and the JNF (ten).[33] The ILA's Director General is an appointee of the government. Thus the JNF, which directly owns 13 per cent of land in Israel, also shapes the policy of the ILA – and this, an organisation that in its own words:

> is not a public body that works for the benefit of all citizens of the state. The loyalty of the JNF is given to the Jewish people and only to them is the JNF obligated. The JNF, as the owner of the JNF land, does not have a duty to practice equality towards all citizens of the state.[34]

A defining moment in legislating for a permanent apartheid was the Basic Law: Israel Lands passed by the Knesset in 1960.[35] Along with the 'Israel Lands Law' passed at the same time, this legislation established a truly comprehensive land regime in Israel for really the first time since 1948.

At the time, the chair of the Constitution, Law and Justice Committee told the Israeli lawmakers that 'the reasons for recommending this law, as far as I understand it, are to provide a legal cover for a principle that at its core is religious, and that is "the land shall never be sold, for the land is mine"' (quoting Leviticus 25:23).[36] A JNF report in 1973 described the 1960 Basic Law as giving 'legal effect to the ancient tradition of ownership of the land in perpetuity by the Jewish people'.[37]

Through the 1950s and into the early 1960s, the Israeli legislature passed laws that regularised the intimate relationship between the state and Zionist institutions like the WZO and the JA.[38] The JA, for example, an explicitly Zionist organisation that exists for the benefit of Jewish people, was given responsibilities normally reserved for the state, with regards to immigration and rural settlement within Israel's 1967 borders.[39]

Another way that Palestinian citizens of Israel are excluded by the apartheid regime is through the 'selection committees' that set the criteria for who can live in almost 70 per cent of Israel's towns.[40] These towns are under the authority of regional councils who have control over around 80 per cent of all the land. Applicants are assessed for 'social suitability' – by a committee made up of government and community representatives, and a senior official of the JA or WZO.

Photograph 5   Palestinians in Israel on an ADRID march in May 2008 (Ben White).

TO BE A PALESTINIAN IN THE JEWISH STATE

The Palestinians who managed to stay inside the borders of the new Israeli state were faced with a shattered society – the majority of their compatriots were now refugees, their property confiscated. Rebuilding after such a trauma was made all the more difficult by the military government the Israeli government maintained over its Palestinian citizens for almost 20 years.

This martial law resembled the kind of all-pervasive intrusion experienced by Palestinians living under military rule in the OPT since 1967. Travel permits, curfews and political arrests were defining characteristics of a regime that for a generation stunted the Arab community's natural growth, prevented the development of an independent political consciousness and fragmented society.

All of which was no accident. Yehoshua Palmon, who in the first years of the Israeli state served under the Minister of Minorities and then as advisor to the Prime Minister on 'Arab affairs', assisted with the day to day running of the military government over the Palestinians. Years later, Palmon described his approach:

> I opposed the integration of Arabs into Israeli society. I preferred separate development...The separation made it possible to maintain a democratic regime within the Jewish population alone.[41]

Another Arab affairs advisor from the 1960s, Uri Lubrani, was frank about the state's relationship to the natives: 'we give them tractors, electricity, and progress, but we take land and restrict their movement ... if they [Arabs] would remain hewers of wood perhaps it would be easier to control them'.[42]

While the military rule over Israel's Palestinian citizens finished in 1966, other fundamental components of the apartheid structure have remained constant to this day. One such characteristic of Israeli state policy is the so-called 'Judaization' of areas where it is deemed there are too many Palestinians and too few Jews, done by confiscating land from Arabs and creating new Jewish settlements. Two particular regions have been the focus of such efforts; the Negev and the Galilee.

One notable example was the creation of Jewish 'Upper Nazareth' overlooking Palestinian Nazareth in the Arab-dominated Galilee. In 1953, one government official crystallised the official thinking of the time:

The only chance of making Nazareth a partially Jewish city is by consolidating the [state] institutions there. It is a colonizing act with difficulties, but without it we will not be able to Judaize Nazareth.[43]

The Israeli government used a law called the 'Land (Acquisition for Public Purposes) Ordinance' in order to confiscate 1,200 dunams in and around Nazareth in 1954, claiming that the seized land would indeed be used in the public interest.[44] In the end, only 9 per cent of the land was used for government offices, with the rest forming the foundations of 'Upper Nazareth'.[45]

Other examples of this 'Judaization' strategy include placing 'lookout' settlements 'around the Galilee to watch over Arab villages' and planting trees 'to guard against Arab encroachment on land'.[46] In 2002, the JA announced major plans to encourage a total of 350,000 Jews to move to the Galilee and Negev, in order to guarantee 'a "Zionist majority" in those areas'.[47] Two years later, the Housing Ministry revealed plans to establish Jewish settlements in the Negev to 'block' the 'expansion' of Bedouin communities.[48]

Racist Israeli state policies are so commonplace that even outside observers can take for granted what in other contexts would be considered absurd or even outrageous. Thus the BBC can note how a Jewish town in the Galilee was set up by the JA 'as a bulwark against the surrounding Israeli Arab villages', or the Washington Post can record that Karmiel emerged as a 'Zionist response to the large Arab population in the Galilee', without outcry.[49]

This is just one way in which the Palestinian citizens of Israel are systematically discriminated against. Between 1957 and 1972, the proportion of the government's total development budget allocated to the Arab sector ranged from 0.2 to 1.5 per cent.[50] By 2008, the budget allocation for Arabs had increased to just 4 per cent, despite the fact that Palestinian citizens are one in five of the population, and half of Arab families are below the poverty line.[51]

Not only do the Palestinians within Israel live as second-class citizens in terms of land ownership and development budgets, but they are also frequently reminded that Israeli society considers their very presence to be a danger. This is commonly referred to as the 'demographic threat', a rather bland expression given that it is used to label Palestinians as dangerous on account of not being Jewish.

Discussing the 'threat' posed by the continued existence of Palestinians within Israel's borders and in the Israeli-controlled OPT is commonplace amongst Israeli politicians, military leaders, academia and the general public. In 2002, the Israeli government reconvened the previously defunct

Demography Council, in order to specifically find solutions to the 'problem'.[52.]

As the Israeli journalist Gideon Levy has pointed out, it is entirely illegitimate to talk of a 'demographic threat': 'Imagine what would happen if a discussion were held in the United States or Europe on "the worrisome natural growth of the Jews"', he points out.[53] Yet this is exactly the kind of language routinely employed to discuss the Palestinians in Israel. In 2005, a drop in the Arab birth rate was viewed as a success to be celebrated, with a senior Finance Ministry official quoted as saying that 'we are reversing the graph, to defend the Jewish majority in the country'.[54]

The *Ha'aretz* report said the drop was 'a clear result of the cutbacks in child support allocations over the past two years', before quickly adding that 'the cutbacks were driven by economic, not demographic reasons'. Just a couple of months later, however, the same newspaper reported that government officials had told the leader of a political party that the reduced child allowance was motivated by 'the desire to reduce the Arab birth-rate'.[55]

In Israel, there is no shame for the most senior of political leaders to describe one group of citizens as a threat on the basis of their ethnicity – as ex-Prime Minister Netanyahu did in 2003 – or to openly discuss how to make sure Israel 'remains Jewish', as then Prime Minister Sharon did in 2005.[56] Press coverage of the latter's remarks noted that Israel's National Security Council had 'recently formulated a plan for "improving the demographic situation in Israel"'. It is in fact no obstacle to a successful political or military career to hold openly racist views regarding the Palestinians.[57]

The racism facing Palestinians in the Jewish state is found in both the legal structure and the rhetoric of political, religious and military leaders. One study in the late 1990s found 20 discriminatory laws, though one of the more strikingly openly racist pieces of legislation is a more recent development.[58] In 2003, the Knesset passed the 'Nationality and Entry into Israel Law' which bans Palestinians from the OPT who marry Israeli citizens from gaining residency or citizenship status.[59]

This 'temporary' law has since been repeatedly renewed by the Knesset, and in 2004 it already affected between 16,000 and 24,000 families, separating husbands and wives from their spouses and children.[60] The legal rights centre Adalah, in a 2008 press release marking yet another extension of the law, noted that 'no other state in the world denies the right to conduct a family life on the basis of national or ethnic belonging'.[61]

There is one final feature of life for a significant number of Palestinians living in the Jewish state that encapsulates their inferior status in political Zionism: legal invisibility. There are two ways in which Palestinians inside Israel and their dwellings are rendered 'invisible': the unrecognised villages and the 'present absentees'.

Unrecognised villages are communities of Palestinians that the Israeli state has refused to officially acknowledge exist.[62] The Planning and Building Law of 1965 categorised the land on which a number of Palestinian villages lay as 'non-residential', thus making their presence illegal: 'the authorities simply pretended they were not there'. With no official status afforded to their communities, the residents receive no government services and their homes are targets for demolition.

It is estimated that there are over 100 such unrecognised villages inside Israel, with the majority concentrated in the south amongst the Bedouin of the Negev.[63] The total number of Arabs affected is around 70–80,000, disconnected from water, electricity, sewerage and the telephone network, and 'prohibited from developing infrastructure'.[64]

There are also thousands of Palestinian individuals who the Israeli state classifies as internal refugees. In 1948, this group left their homes and towns but remained in what became Israel. Yet under Israeli legislation, having been 'absent' from their home for even a short period of time, they lost their land and property. So although citizens, these Palestinians 'were forcibly prevented from reasserting possession over property declared to have been "abandoned"', and are called 'present absentees'.[65]

Around one in four Palestinian citizens of Israel are 'present absentees'.[66] The battle of the residents of two villages, Kafr Bir'im and Iqrit, to return home is instructive about the relationship between Israeli apartheid and the native Arabs.[67] Originally evicted by the Israeli army in November 1948, the Christian Palestinian villagers were assured that their removal was for 'temporary' security purposes.

By 1951, the villagers had still not been allowed home, and so they filed a claim in the Israeli High Court of Justice. Three months later, the army declared Kafr Bir'im a 'closed' military area requiring special permits for entry, and then in December, with the case still before the court, the army detonated every house in Iqrit. In 1953, the remaining houses of Kafr Bir'im were destroyed by the army. The lands of both villages were confiscated, declared 'state lands', and made available for Jewish development.

Since then, the persistence of the villagers has occasionally raised the profile of their case. In the mid 1990s, a government committee suggested a deal that the villagers rejected on the grounds that it severely restricted both the numbers allowed back and the amount of land to be recovered. When the case has come before the Israeli cabinet, such as in 1972 and 2001, the response has been the same: the villagers are refused permission to return on the grounds of 'security', and out of fear that it would set a 'precedent' for the other Palestinian present absentees.

PALESTINIANS INSIDE ISRAEL: CONCLUSION

Perhaps the core of Israeli apartheid as it affects the country's Palestinian citizens is the 'exclusionary land regime', a reflection of the historic objective of political Zionism: the land of Palestine without the Palestinians.[68] The three main tools of this regime are: physical dispossession; the system for 'the ownership and administration' of 'public' land; and the bureaucratic arrangements 'regulating land development and land-use planning'. The open racism faced by Palestinian citizens of Israel is simply a result of the central contradiction inherent in the idea of a 'Jewish democratic' state.

THE OCCUPATION

As mentioned briefly at the end of Part I, the necessity of the ethnic cleansing of the indigenous Palestinians presented Israel with a challenge after it occupied the rest of Palestine in 1967 (the West Bank, East Jerusalem and Gaza Strip). Excepting mass expulsions (unfeasible in terms of Israel's international relations and regional context), Israel would have to live with a massive Palestinian majority in the OPT. In order to maintain dominance over land access and natural resources therefore, and in order to keep the Palestinians fragmented and weakened, Israel had to develop an apartheid regime in the occupied territories far more explicit than what had already been in place since 1948.

Israel was faced with a problem, however, in that the international community viewed the Palestinian territories conquered in 1967 as occupied and only under temporary Israeli control, pending a peace agreement. International and humanitarian law also laid out strict provisions for what an occupying power could or could not do in the territory under control.

Faced with these obstacles, maintaining an apartheid regime to control the Palestinians had to be a gradual, unspoken and duplicitous process. Sometimes Israel has simply ignored what weak international protest emerged; other times Israel has resorted to legal fictions, or encouraged a religiously radical settler movement whose 'outposts' turn into official colonies. Most commonly, Israel resorted to hiding behind the excuse of 'security' considerations, slowing down or speeding up the pace of the colonisation according to 'peace process' sensitivities or periods of Palestinian violence.

During the last 40 years, Israel has effectively integrated the conquered area with the pre 1967 territory, through a 'matrix of control' that incorporates Jewish colonies, settler-only roads, checkpoints, military bases, no-go zones and water resources.[69] The following is an overview of the mechanisms and characteristics of Israeli apartheid in the OPT.

LAND THEFT

We enthusiastically chose to become a colonial society ... engaging in theft and finding justification for all these activities.

Michael Ben-Yair, March 2002[70]

The main characteristic of Israel's rule in the OPT since 1967 has been land theft. Israel has tried to veil its rapacious land seizures with a veneer of legality and 'due process'. Thus in the aftermath of the 1967 war, the Israeli military introduced a number of 'Military Orders' designed to ease the takeover of Palestinian property.[71]

Israel has replicated inside the OPT many of the same land confiscation policies and laws that it used after 1948.[72] There was an added impetus after 1979, when 'government agencies started a large-scale project of mapping and land registration in order to discover public lands to which Israel could lay claim'.[73] If a Palestinian could not prove private ownership *and* present use (i.e. public Palestinian land), it was seized.

An Amnesty International report in 1999 detailed how successive Israeli governments have manipulated the question of 'public land' for massive scale colonisation, including the cynical way in which Israeli authorities depend on Ottoman land legislation dating back to 1858.[74] Even more cynically, Palestinians have been subjected to discrimination based on prohibiting 'alien persons' from 'building on or renting state lands'. Ironically, while immigrants under the Law of Return (i.e. Jews) are given full rights, the definition of 'alien' includes almost the entire Palestinian population in areas occupied after 1967.

The pace of Israeli colonisation has varied, though both Likud *and* Labor governments have aggressively pursued substantial confiscation policies. Moreover, even during the years of the Oslo 'peace process', the Israeli government confiscated around 35,000 acres in the West Bank, 'much of it agricultural and worth more than $1 billion', in order to expand the settlements and build their bypass roads.[75] Between 1995 and 1999, Israel confiscated land equivalent to the size of London every year.[76]

By the mid 1980s, Palestinian cultivated land in the West Bank had dropped by 40 per cent.[77] By the spring of 2000, six months before the Second Intifada began, the Special Rapporteur for the UN's Commission on Human Rights estimated that since 1967, Israel had confiscated 60 per cent of the West Bank, a third of the Gaza Strip and a third of Palestinian land in Jerusalem.[78]

Nabil Saba

'In 1972 the Israeli soldiers came to my family's home at the top of Beit Jala, and offered to buy the land from my father. We refused. So almost every day and night they would come to the house, to threaten us, to intimidate us. They would take me and my brothers to jail. They falsely accused us of supporting the guerrillas with 300 dinars, which was a lot of money in those days. They beat my brother in jail.

The Israelis would come to our home and put me and my brothers up against a wall. Then they would ask my mother which one of us she wants to see killed first. My mother would cry. After a year, we left the house, taking most of our belongings with us. We thought we would be away just temporarily; we left out of fear.

The soldiers came and demanded the keys. They wanted to occupy one room in the house, they said, to stop the guerrillas. After that, they stopped us going back to the house. I've never been back since.

If I were to go back, I would have a heart attack to see Israeli housing there. There were grapes, fig trees; they were all bulldozed, like you see them doing to the olive trees. My father, before he died, said he wished he could sleep just one more night in his house. I will never forget those words.'

Source: Interview with author.

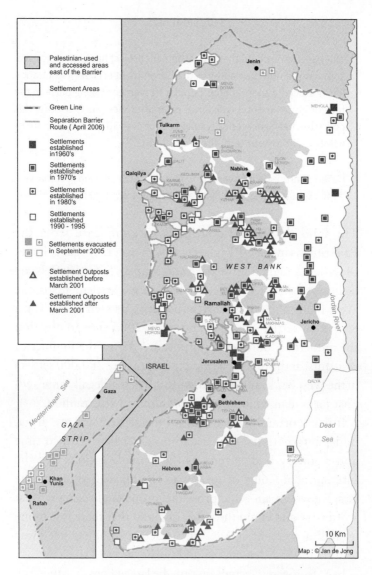

Map 3 Settlements established and evacuated 1967–2008

Source: Foundation for Middle East Peace.

SETTLEMENTS

There seems no doubt that the settlement project has been conceived, stimulated and implemented by the Government of Israel; colonization has not been a spontaneous popular movement taking place in the face of governmental resistance or indifference. Furthermore, this policy has been energetically followed for over 30 years by all administrations from 1967 until the present time.[79]

[Ariel] Sharon, flying over the Occupied Territories once remarked: 'Arabs should see Jewish lights every night from 500 metres.'[80]

The land that Israel continues to confiscate from the Palestinians in the OPT is largely given over to illegal colonies of settlers and their infrastructure (Map 3). Since 1967, Israel has established 135 officially recognised settlements in the West Bank (including East Jerusalem), as well as the Gaza Strip's 16 settlements dismantled in 2005 (not to mention the numerous 'unofficial' outposts).[81] As for the number of residents, at the time of writing there are over 280,000 settlers in the West Bank, and more than 180,000 in (illegally annexed) East Jerusalem, making a total of almost half a million.[82]

It is important to note that all the settlements are illegal under international law, a damning verdict returned time and again by bodies such as the United Nations and the International Court of Justice at The Hague. Although the Israeli government – and pro-Israel propagandists in the West – often try and cloud the issue, or claim that there is genuine legal disagreement, in 1967 the Israeli government itself was told that the settlements would be illegal.

In a 'Top Secret' memorandum, the Israeli Foreign Ministry's legal counsel concluded that 'civilian settlement in the administered territories contravenes the explicit provisions of the Fourth Geneva Convention', noting that the prohibition is 'categorical and is not conditioned on the motives or purposes of the transfer, and is aimed at preventing colonization of conquered territory by citizens of the conquering state'.[83]

Israel has carefully planned the location of important settlements, often grouping colonies together to form 'blocs' in strategic locations, especially around Jerusalem. In 1983, the World Zionist Organization and the Ministry of Agriculture prepared a settlement 'Master Plan' that 'envisaged the eventual incorporation of the West Bank into Israel, aiming "to disperse maximally large Jewish population in areas of high settlement priority..."'.[84] The goal, then, of these 'facts on the ground' is to create areas that Israel can eventually annex.

Sometimes it is assumed that settlement construction has been mainly driven by the Israeli political 'right', especially the religious zealots. In fact, over the decades there has been a remarkable consensus across the spectrum. For example, by the time that Labor left power ten years after the 1967 war, 'about 50,000 Israeli Jews were already settled in the new Jewish neighbourhoods established on the peripheries of the occupied areas annexed to Jerusalem'.[85]

What Labor started, Likud enthusiastically continued, more than doubling the number of settlements and almost quadrupling the settler population in the government's first term of office.[86] However, one would have thought that, at least after the 1993 Oslo Accords, there would be a halt, if not reduction, in Israeli colonisation. In fact, in the years that followed, the number of settlers *doubled* – including a 50 per cent rise to 147,000 settlers between 1993 and 1996 when Labor was in power.[87]

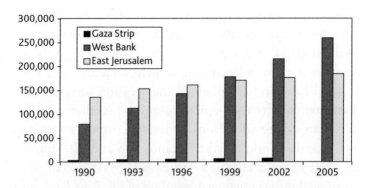

Chart 3   Settler population growth in the OPT, 1990–2005

Source: FMEP, http://fmep.org/settlement_info/settlement-info-and-tables/stats-data/
comprehensive-settlement-population-1972-2006.

Photograph 6   Har Homa settlement, outside Bethlehem in the West Bank,
May 2008 (Ben White).

Daoud Nassar

'We have been fighting to keep our land from the Israeli military since 1991. If anyone "claimed" to own the land he had to go and present his case to a military court. Some had no papers or documents to prove ownership and so lost their land.

When the [Second] intifada started the settlers wanted to confiscate the land. Sometimes they came with machine guns. One time I showed a settler my papers showing ownership of the land, and he said that he had papers from God. They tried to open a road through the land, they uprooted our trees, pulled down fences, broke water tanks, but we just kept mending everything. Now we try and keep a permanent presence here.

Our project here is called "Tent of Nations", a place to bring different religions, cultures and nationalities together. There are a lot of projects in Area A and B but this is not where it is important to do something. If we don't do something like this in Area C then the land might just be taken one day.'

Source: Interview with author.

'BYPASS ROADS'

The roads regime, which is based on separation through discrimina-tion, bears clear similarities to the racist apartheid regime that existed in South Africa until 1994.[88]

B'Tselem report, 2004

An integral part of Israeli colonisation in the OPT is the network of bypass roads that link up colonies and further fragment Palestinian land. By 2000, these roads had a total length of 340 km and took up 51.2 square km in the West Bank.[89] Jeff Halper, of the Israeli Committee Against Home Demolitions, has described how these bypass roads are 'lined on both sides with "sanitary" margins that eliminate all Palestinian homes, fields and orchards in their path', incorporating 'the West Bank into Israel's national highway system'.[90]

The bypass roads, intended to serve Israeli citizens rather than Palestinians, are governed according to a discriminatory regime ranging from banning Palestinians to partial restrictions like physical obstacles and/or special permits.[91] In 2005 and 2006, new Israeli plans surfaced for the 'upgrade' of the bypass system, 'creating a Palestinian state of enclaves, surrounded by walls and linked by tunnels and special roads'. This 'would create an "apartheid" road network for Palestinians in the West Bank' whereby 'existing roads would be reserved for Jews, linking their settlements to each other and to Israel'.[92]

At around the same time, practical steps began to be taken by the Israeli occupation authorities to enforce the separation, with the Israeli military blocking 'Palestinians from driving on the main artery through the West Bank'. Apparently, the government approved plan would culminate in the barring of 'all Palestinians from roads used by Israelis in the West Bank', the purpose being 'total separation between the two populations'.[93]

By 2008, Israel was finding it hard to keep up even the pretence of democracy. For the first time in its history, the High Court of Justice issued an interim decision on a specific road (Route 443) that meant the closing of a road in the OPT to Palestinians, purely 'for the convenience of Israeli travellers'.[94] In an article about the 'two-tier road system', the New York Times quoted Limor Yehuda, attorney for The Association for Civil Rights in Israel, mentioning that word – 'apartheid'.[95]

Photograph 7 Bypass road south of Jerusalem, with olive trees ready for removal, July 2006 (Ben White).

Photograph 8 Palestinian man with his ID and Israeli military travel permission slip (Andy Sims, http://www.andysimsphotography.com).

Photograph 9   Rubble placed by the IDF to block Palestinian access, west of
Bethlehem, May 2008 (Ben White).

CHECKPOINTS AND CLOSURE

The checkpoint system belongs entirely to the Israeli unwillingness
to give up all of the territory of the West Bank, including all of the
settlements. The checkpoint system is aimed at ensuring Israeli
control over the lives of the Palestinians.[96]

Yitzhak Laor

[The checkpoints'] function is to send a message of force and
authority, to inspire fear, and to symbolize the downtrodden nature
and inferiority of those under the occupation.[97]

Meron Benvenisti

Across the OPT there are hundreds of Israeli obstacles to
Palestinian freedom of movement, from manned checkpoints
to blocked roads and iron gates. The majority of these

obstacles, including major, permanently manned checkpoints, are not on the Green Line, but rather restrict or completely prevent the free flow of pedestrians and traffic from one Palestinian town and city to another. The United Nations painstakingly documents the quantity and type of obstacles, which also include trenches, earth mounds, the Separation Wall (more later) and random or 'flying' checkpoints.

In May 2008, the UN's Office for the Coordination of Humanitarian Affairs (OCHA) in Jerusalem estimated there to be 607 obstacles in the West Bank, which was a 7 per cent increase from the previous September.[98] OCHA also pointed out how 'these measures are frequently implemented in an unpredictable way', meaning that 'the total number of closure obstacles present at a given time, although indicative, does not fully capture the relative severity of the closure regime'.[99]

Israel claims that the checkpoints are there to fight terrorism. It is difficult, however, to understand what 'security' rationale there can be for preventing Palestinians from reaching their own weddings or blocking a village's only access road. An editorial in *Ha'aretz*, however, suggested that 'encirclement, or more bluntly, siege, of Palestinian villages' lacking 'even a pretense of having a security purpose' is in fact, 'a real tool of severe and collective punishment'.[100]

The checkpoints and other obstacles are one way that Israel enforces the policy of 'closure' on the occupied Palestinians, a series of 'restrictions placed on the free movement of Palestinian people, vehicles and goods'.[101] Enforced 'by a complex bureaucratic-military travel permit system and a two-colour car licence plates system', 'closure' can be: internal (of towns and villages in the OPT); external (of the border between Israel and the OPT); or external including international crossings.

Contrary to the claim by some that this kind of collective punishment only became necessary with the suicide bombings of the Second Intifada, closure has been imposed by Israel on the OPT 'since the early 1990s', and 'is much too far-reaching to be seen as an ad hoc measure linked to Palestinian security performance'.[102] Between 1994 and 1999, Israel imposed a total of 499 days of closure; while by 1998, less than 4 per cent of Palestinians from the West Bank and Gaza Strip had permission to enter Jerusalem.[103]

Shaza Younis

'I am a student at university in Nablus. But my family and I live in Jenin, and so I must make the difficult journey to Nablus through Israeli checkpoints. I never know how long it will take me to make this journey each time. Once, I left Jenin in the middle of the afternoon, and reached the checkpoint. Hundreds of cars were waiting, and the weather was so cold, so we continued walking to reach the other side. When I reached the soldiers, one of them suddenly pushed me down to the ground, claiming that I crossed the line. Then another Palestinian man walked forward and pushed this soldier, and so many soldiers attacked him, hitting him, and then taking him away – where I don't know.'

Source: Interview with author.

THE SEPARATION WALL

The course of the wall clearly indicates that its purpose is to incorporate as many settlers as possible into Israel.[104]

> John Dugard, law professor and UN Special Rapporteur to
> the Human Rights Council on the Human Rights Situation
> in the Occupied Palestinian Territory

In 2003, Israel began work on the Separation Wall in the West Bank and East Jerusalem, a major development in the geography and control mechanisms of the occupation. The International Court of Justice's (ICJ) advisory ruling (see below) explained that the term 'Wall' was satisfactory, though in different places it features a 25 feet high wall, razor wire, trenches, sniper

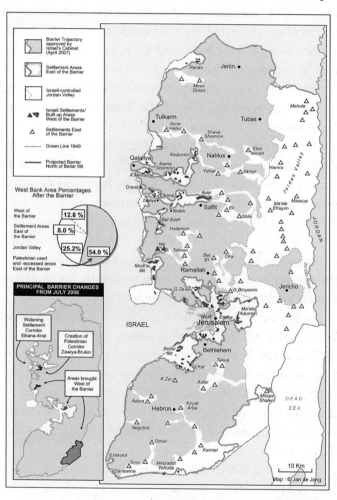

Map 4   Israel's Wall and settlements (colonies) February 2007

Source: PLO's Negotiation Affairs Department

towers, electrified fences, military roads, electronic surveillance and buffer zones of up to 100 metres in width.[105]

The current route of the Wall is over 720 km in length, which as of May 2008 was 57 per cent complete, with 9 per cent under construction.[106] Around 75 per cent of the total length of the projected Wall lies inside the West Bank, with 10 per cent of West Bank and East Jerusalem land being caught between the Barrier and the Green Line.[107] The tens of thousands of Palestinians trapped in this 'no man's land' are isolated from the rest of the West Bank and require 'permission' to stay in their homes.[108]

The Separation Wall is also illegal. In a landmark case, the ICJ at The Hague ruled in July 2004 by 14 to 1 that 'the construction of the wall being built by Israel, the occupying power, in the occupied Palestinian territory, including in and around East Jerusalem, and its associated regime, are contrary to international law'.[109] The ICJ also ruled (14–1) that Israel is obliged to stop the Wall's construction, dismantle what has already been done, and 'make reparation for all damage caused by the construction of the wall'.

The ICJ decision came after the Separation Wall had already been condemned by numerous human rights organisations, including the International Committee of the Red Cross, who in an unusually strong statement in February 2004 denounced the Wall as '"contrary" to international law'.[110] Amnesty International had already given their view the year before: construction of the Wall 'must be halted immediately' they said.[111]

The main justification given by the Israeli government and its apologists for the Wall is security, and specifically, Palestinian suicide bombers. Even as a 'security measure', the Wall is of debatable significance. For example, in late 2007, over 1,200 Palestinians were bypassing the Wall to work without permits in Israel on average *every week*.[112] While the Wall has contributed to a sharp drop in Palestinian attacks inside Israel, the Israeli security service itself attributed this improvement in 2006 to the ceasefire unilaterally implemented by Palestinian armed groups.[113]

The collective punishment of a population in the name of 'security' is, of course, expressly forbidden by the Geneva Conventions. Yet the best answer to those who pretend, like Sharon, that 'the terror built the fence', is to produce a map of the route.[114] The Wall's path does not lie on Israel's border with the OPT, but instead loops around to include the most important colonies on the 'Israeli' side. According to data from Israel's Interior Ministry, more than 75 per cent of all settlers will be included to the west of the Wall, by its present route (Map 4).[115]

The logic of the Wall is to grab as much land as possible, with as few Palestinians as possible. That is according to the Wall's main designer, Danny Tirza, who told the *Washington Post* in 2007 that 'the main thing the government told me in giving me the job was to include as many Israelis inside the fence and leave as many Palestinians outside'.[116] Tirza is himself a settler, 'who believes Israel has a historic right to the land between the Mediterranean Sea and the Jordan River'.

The Wall has had a devastating effect on Palestinians' ability to maintain their way of life. Neighbouring villages are now hours away, or completely unreachable. The first phase land grab alone, in the northern district of the West Bank, was 95 per cent prime agricultural land, including citrus and olive trees, cropland and pasture.[117] The land closed off by the Wall contains, 'coincidentally', 65 per cent of the West Bank Palestinians' water sources.[118]

Jayyous is one village that has been particularly affected by the Wall. David Bloom described in a piece for *The Nation* in 2004 how 'seventy percent of the villagers' farmland – and all their irrigated land – has ended up on the western side of Israel's 'security fence'.[119] The physical separation has paved the way for progressive, bureaucratic dispossession:

> Once, 300 Jayyous farmers went to their lands every day. Then the wall was built. At first the gates were open. Then the Israelis placed locks and chains on them. Then they started locking the gates, only opening them for about fifteen or twenty minutes at a time. On October 2 the Israeli West Bank military commander, Gen. Moshe Kaplinsky, declared the area between the wall and the Green Line to be a closed military zone .... [and] the rules of the seam zone require that no Palestinian can enter without a permit issued by Israel. However, Israeli citizens and those eligible to be citizens under the Law of Return are allowed to enter.

Photograph 10   The Separation Wall in Bethlehem, September 2005
(Andy Sims, http://www.andysimsphotography.com).

The situation in Jayyous is part of the 'new geographical and bureaucratic reality' created by the Wall 'for hundreds of thousands of Palestinians in the northern West Bank'.[120] But it's not just the north of the OPT; in East Jerusalem, an enormous concrete wall slices through Palestinian neighbourhoods, while in Bethlehem, the north of the city has been turned into a ghost town.

EAST JERUSALEM

[Israel's] main concern seems to be to ensure that this conquest of Jerusalem be the last one.

The Economist[121]

We break up Arab continuity and their claim to East Jerusalem by putting in isolated islands of Jewish presence in areas of Arab population... Our eventual goal is Jewish continuity in all of Jerusalem.[122]

Uri Bank, Moledet party

After capturing East Jerusalem in 1967, Israel moved quickly to make the conquest an unquestionable – and irreversible – fact on the ground. The very same month, the Israeli parliament passed legislation extending Jerusalem's municipal boundaries to include the newly occupied territory.[123] This act of effective annexation has never been recognised as legal by the international community.

The annexation amounted to over 1,700 acres of East Jerusalem and the West Bank, and around a third of the land was also expropriated – most of it privately owned Palestinian property.[124] This land was then used for illegal settlement construction; by 2001, around 47,000 housing units had been built for Jews on this expropriated land – 'but not one unit for Palestinians'.[125]

A key Israeli goal in Jerusalem is to increase the proportion of the Jewish population, though until now, one in three of the city's residents are Palestinian (this increases to over 50 per cent on land annexed in 1967).[126] In order to win the 'demographic' battle, Israel physically isolates East Jerusalem from the West Bank, discriminates in land and housing plans, revokes Palestinian residency rights and neglects East Jerusalem infrastructure.[127]

Amir Cheshin served as Senior Advisor on Arab Community Affairs and Assistant to Teddy Kollek, mayor of Jerusalem from 1965 to 1993. In his book, he gives an insider's perspective on Israel's racist discrimination, writing how:

> the 1970 Kollek plan contains the principles upon which Israeli housing policy in east Jerusalem is based to this day – expropriation of Arab-owned land, development of large Jewish neighbourhoods in east Jerusalem, and limitations on development in Arab neighbourhoods.[128]

Thus when Ariel Sharon dedicated a new house of Jewish families in the Old City's Muslim Quarter in 1992, declaring, 'We have set a goal for ourselves of not leaving one neighbourhood in East Jerusalem without Jews', he was not speaking as an 'extremist' individual, but as a man in tune with official policy.[129]

The Palestinians of East Jerusalem have different identity cards to West Bank Palestinians. They are not Israeli citizens, but are under Israeli law, considered 'residents'.[130] Furthermore, their 'right' to residency can be revoked by Israel, if certain criteria are not met; in 2006 alone, over 1,300 East Jerusalem Palestinians had their residency rights revoked.[131] In this way, '"Israel treats them like other non-naturalised immigrants, 'though it was Israel, in effect, that immigrated to them"'.[132]

Since so much land is deliberately 'off-limits' for Palestinian development, there is a huge housing shortage (in stark contrast to the willingness with which the Israeli government expands or initiates illegal Jewish colonies). Palestinians are also routinely denied permission to build, and are 'therefore faced with a choice': either build and risk demolition, or buy outside the municipality and 'in so doing lose their status as citizens of Jerusalem'.[133] Between 2004 and 2007, 316 Palestinian homes built without permits were demolished, leaving almost 1,000 people homeless.[134]

WATER

Since the military occupation began in 1967, the Palestinians have been systematically discriminated against when it comes to accessing and using the water resources of their own land. On an annual per capita basis, 'Israelis consume more than four times as much water as Palestinians', while the aquifer that is the only water source for West Bank residents is left with only 17 per cent for Palestinian usage, after Israel takes the rest for its own cities and settlements.[135]

The Israeli military authorities have 'largely forbidden Palestinians from drilling new wells or rehabilitating old ones', as well as enforcing restrictions on the depth Palestinian pumps are allowed to reach down to – restrictions, of course, that do not exist for the settlements.[136] The settlements in fact continue to play a double role in denying Palestinians access to their water resources.

Firstly, the settlers use hugely disproportionate amounts of water, compared to the Palestinian towns and villages around them. In the heat of the summer in 1997, for example, the settlers of the Kiryat Arba colony were allocated more than eight times as much water per person as the Hebron Palestinians forced to live alongside this group of extremists protected by an occupation army.[137]

Secondly, the very location of the colonies is related to Israel's intentions of permanently holding on to those parts of the West Bank that would grant control over water resources like aquifers. In an interview in 2001, Ariel Sharon admitted that 'it's not by accident that the settlements are located where they are', adding that 'come what may' Israel must hold on to territory including the 'hill aquifer'.[138] Marwan Bishara, a Palestinian writer and researcher, noted that 'the map of the settlements looked like a hydraulic map of the territories'.[139]

DETENTION AND TORTURE

In light of the large number of those arrested and detained for a short time with very little interrogation, and the consistent use of degrading treatment, Amnesty International is concerned that the aim of the large-scale arrests may have been to collectively punish and to degrade and humiliate Palestinians not involved in armed opposition.[140]

Amnesty International, May 2002

Israel administratively detains Palestinians for their political opinions and non-violent political activity.[141]

B'Tselem

In the last four decades, around 700,000 Palestinians have at one time or another been detained by Israel, including almost

50,000 during the Second Intifada.[142] During 'Operation Defensive Shield' in 2002, the Israeli army detained around 15,000 Palestinians across the West Bank, 6,000 of whom were still in prison by the end of 2003.[143] The number of prisoners, who are mostly held in jails inside Israel rather than the Occupied Territories, of course varies. In September 2006, B'Tselem estimated the number to be 'more than 9,000', while a *Reuters* report in May 2008 put the figure at around 11,000.[144]

Taken from their home or workplace by an occupation army, some Palestinians are not even able to defend the charges brought against them. That is because Israel holds hundreds of Palestinians under 'administrative detention', a polite name for keeping someone prisoner 'without trying them and without informing them of the suspicions against them'.[145]

Military commanders in the West Bank can detain someone 'for up to six months if they have "reasonable grounds to presume that the security of the area or public security require the detention"', the interpretation of which is left to the army.[146] This sentence can be renewed every six months, indefinitely, while the hearing is carried out without the detainee or their attorney being privy to the evidence. The number of Palestinians being held by Israel in administrative detention at any given time fluctuates; sometimes it is over 1,000, and it rarely drops below 500. In February 2008, the figure was around 780.[147]

Palestinian prisoners are routinely abused, both during their initial capture as well as in detention. In fact, it was only in 1999 that the Israeli High Court of Justice ruled against the use of torture during interrogations.[148] But a crucial loophole was left, meaning that security agents would not be held criminally responsible for applying prohibited 'physical pressure' if 'it is subsequently found that the methods were used in a "ticking-bomb" case'.[149]

Human Rights Watch noted that in 2002, the Israeli General Security Service (GSS) 'had up to that point employed "exceptional interrogation means" against ninety Palestinians':

> The readiness of the Attorney General to grant 'necessity defense' requests, along with the fact that since 1999 no Israeli Security Agency or GSS officer has faced criminal or disciplinary charges for acts of torture or ill-treatment, appears to have led to an erosion of the restraints initially imposed by the 1999 ruling.[150]

So while the 1999 court decision made a significant difference, it comes as no surprise that a May 2007 detainees' survey by two Israeli human rights groups found that interrogations by Israeli Security Agency personnel 'routinely included mental and physical ill-treatment'.[151]

HOME DEMOLITIONS

> The demolition of Palestinian houses is inextricably linked with Israeli policy to control and colonize areas of the West Bank.[152]
>
> Amnesty International, 1999

The demolition of Palestinian homes has always been part of the occupation. In 1971, 2,000 houses in Gaza were cleared under the command of Ariel Sharon 'to facilitate military control'.[153] During the First Intifada of the late 1980s to early 1990s, over 2,000 houses were destroyed, while in the Oslo 'peace process' years, almost 1,700 'illegal' Palestinian homes were demolished by court order.

Yet it was during the Second Intifada that home demolition truly became a weapon in Israel's war against the Palestinians. Between September 2000 and May 2007, an estimated 5,000 Palestinian homes were destroyed in military operations, with tens of thousands of others left uninhabitable.[154] Sometimes there are bursts of intense destruction, such as in May 2004, when '298 buildings were demolished and 3,800 people were made homeless' in the Gaza Strip.[155] Almost 9 per cent of Rafah's population lost their homes in the first four years of the Second Intifada.[156]

By May 2007, 'about 1900 Palestinian homes have been demolished by the Civil Administration for lack of proper

---

Fatima al-Ghanami

'They came at 10 o'clock in the morning. They didn't notify us the day before in order to let us prepare. They came at the house from behind, not from the front. They took everything out – all the furniture and utensils, all our belongings. The house had four rooms and a bathroom and it cost 70,000 NIS to build. We couldn't do anything, we were totally helpless. Some of my sons were here, but they didn't protest or resist because we all knew that no matter what we did they'd demolish the house anyway. We also had to pay for a bulldozer to come and remove the mess they left of the ruined home. That cost us 700 NIS right there. Afterwards my sons built me this temporary shack, but now it also has a demolition order...When I got the first demolition order for the old house I was sure they would never come. Now I know better. I know they'll come and do it.... They might come tomorrow, they might come anytime. If they demolish this place I have nowhere to go and no money left. I have no idea what I'll do.'

Source: Human Rights Watch interview, from 'Off the map: land and housing rights violations in Israel's unrecognized Bedouin villages', March 2008.

permits' and over 600 homes were demolished as punishment (the latter practice ceasing in 2005).[157] A UN report in May 2008 revealed that in the previous seven years, Israel denied 94 per cent of Palestinian building permit requests in the more than 60 per cent of the West Bank under direct Israeli military and administrative authority.[158]

Amnesty International documented how 'house demolitions are usually carried out without warning, often at night, and the occupants are forcibly evicted with no time to salvage their belongings. Often the only warning is the rumbling of the Israeli army's US-made Caterpillar bulldozers beginning to tear down the walls of their homes'.[159]

MILITARY BRUTALITY

Like all occupations, Israel's was founded on brute force, repression and fear, collaboration and treachery, beatings and torture chambers, and daily intimidation, humiliation, and manipulation.[160]

Benny Morris

Since the beginning of the occupation in 1967, Israel has regularly needed to suppress Palestinian resistance with military force. During the First Intifada (uprising), 1987–93, Israeli security forces killed over 1,000 Palestinians, one in five of them children.[161] A third of this eventual death toll had already been reached after nine months.[162] Around the world, people watched the images of occupying soldiers breaking the bones of Palestinians, responding to civil disobedience and stone throwing with beatings and bullets.

The Second Intifada, however, which began in September 2000, saw Israel deploying its military on a far greater scale. In the first few days of the Palestinian uprising known as the

Second Intifada, and 'before the wave of terror attacks against Israelis even began', the Israeli army fired 1.3 million bullets, a statistic that casts doubt on the claim that IDF violence is a 'regrettable but necessary' response to Palestinian terror (Chart 4). [163] As Derek Gregory points out, with the outbreak of rioting and protests by the occupied Palestinians,

> The IDF responded with astonishing violence; no Israeli civilians were killed by Palestinians until November, but by October Israel had already deployed high-velocity bullets, helicopter gunships, tanks, and missiles against the Palestinian population.[164]

From 29 September 2000 to the end of May 2008, over 5,100 Palestinians were killed by Israeli forces (Chart 5).[165] Over 1,000 Israelis died in Palestinian attacks. To get some kind of perspective on the scale of Palestinian fatalities, the US equivalent would be the violent deaths of 385,000 people – or more than 120 '9/11's.

Some periods saw particularly high casualties, such as during Operation Defensive Shield in 2002 – the largest military operation in the West Bank since the 1967 war. Launched at the end of March after a string of bloody Palestinian suicide bombings, the Israeli army invaded the major Palestinian cities like Bethlehem, Ramallah, Nablus and Jenin, deploying tanks, bulldozers and helicopter gunships.

In a period of three weeks, around 500 Palestinians were killed and 1,500 were injured.[166] The operation was characterised by extensive curfews, the systematic destruction of Palestinian Authority infrastructure, and various documented human rights abuses and war crimes.[167]

The Gaza Strip has witnessed some of the most devastating IDF attacks and the worst human rights abuses. In May 2004, the Israeli military killed 45 Palestinians (including

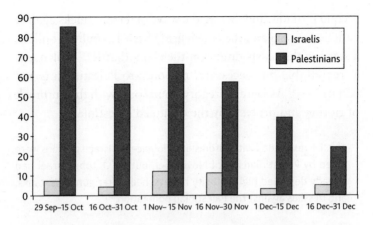

Chart 4   Second Intifada deaths, 29 September 2000–31 December 2000
Source: Middle East Policy Council, http://www.mepc.org.

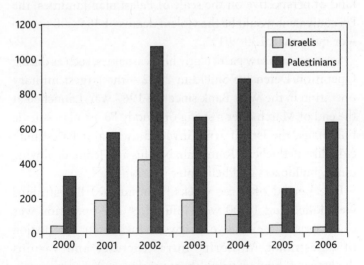

Chart 5   Second Intifada deaths, 2000–2006
Source: Middle East Policy Council.

38 civilians), and in six days made 575 people homeless.[168] Less than six months later, 'Operation Days of Penitence' saw more than 30 Palestinian children killed by Israeli forces in the first two weeks.[169] In the summer of 2006, after an Israeli soldier was captured by Palestinian fighters, Israel launched attacks that killed over 200 Palestinians in two months (including 44 children).[170]

During the years of the Second Intifada, there were numerous documented cases of the deliberate murder of Palestinian civilians – including many children – by Israeli soldiers. Between September 2000 and May 2004, 545 Palestinian children were killed by Israeli forces or settlers; almost half of whom were under the age of 14. Nearly 1,500 had sustained life-long disabilities. Some observers have concluded that the Israeli army was killing civilians 'knowingly and deliberately':

> One of these organisations is Physicians for Human Rights-USA, which investigated the number of Palestinian deaths and injuries in the first months of the Intifada. It concluded that 'the pattern of injuries seen in many victims did not reflect IDF use of firearms in life-threatening situations but rather indicated targeting solely for the purpose of wounding or killing'.[171]

In Rafah, May 2004, siblings Asma and Ahmad al-Mughayr, aged 16 and 13 respectively, were both killed with a bullet to the head 'within minutes of each other on the roof-terrace of their home' as they took clothes off the drying line and fed the pigeons.[172] In a typical kind of response, the Israeli army immediately claimed that Asma and Ahmad had been killed by an explosion caused by Palestinian fighters. It is only when specific cases are investigated – normally by human rights groups or journalists – that the true facts come to light, and the IDF is forced to change its story.

On the rare occasion that the death of a Palestinian civilian is officially investigated, Israeli soldiers typically either escape discipline entirely, or receive a token, disproportionate punishment. One Israeli soldier later revealed that in his unit the attitude was, 'so kids got killed. For a soldier it means nothing. An officer can get a 100 or 200 shekel [£12.50–£25] fine for such a thing.'[173]

A particularly striking incident was the murder of 13-year-old Iman al-Hams, a schoolgirl from Rafah. In October 2004, she entered an area declared out of bounds by the Israeli army and shortly afterwards was riddled with bullets from automatic gunfire. Soldiers present at the time described how their commanding officer 'confirmed' the kill by shooting her in the head and emptying his magazine into her body.[174]

While this incident seems exceptional for its cold-blooded brutality, a B'Tselem staff member pointed out that 'disregard for human life and being trigger-happy is not exceptional at all' and that 'the exceptional part here is that it was documented'. In the end, the army acquitted the commander of Iman's death, accepting his defence that 'he fired into the ground near the girl after coming under fire in a dangerous area' – though without explaining 'why the officer shot into the ground rather than at the source of the fire'.[175]

In an extra twist, the commander in question was later *compensated* to the tune of over £10,000, as well as having all legal expenses reimbursed.[176] *Ha'aretz* noted that 'the judges who acquitted Captain R accepted his version of event [sic], in which he stated that the shots that he fired were not aimed directly at the girl's body... and that he believed that the young girl posed a serious threat'. He has since been promoted to major.

During the Second Intifada, the Israeli military has also targeted the very fabric of Palestinian political, social and economic life. During Operation Defensive Shield, for example, the 'civilian infrastructure' of the Palestinian Authority was targeted, with the ransacking of PA ministries, the confiscation of hard disks, 'the burning of files and, more bizarrely, the wrecking of bathroom fixtures and upholstery'.[177] On several occasions, 'faeces were left in ministers' offices'.

Early in the Second Intifada, Palestinian boy Mohammad Al-Dura was filmed being shot to death, apparently by Israeli soldiers. Since then, the video has been the focus of a dispute over an alleged manipulation of the footage. But writing in *Ha'aretz*, Gideon Levy pointed out the pettiness of the

Photograph 11   The morning after an Israeli raid, Balata refugee camp, near Nablus, September 2006 (Ben White).

obsession with the Al-Dura film, when the general pattern
of the murder of children is taken into account:

> Al-Dura became a symbol because his killing was documented on
> videotape. All the other hundreds of children were killed without
> cameras present, so no one is interested in their fate. If there had
> been a camera in Bushara Barjis' room in the Jenin refugee camp while
> she was studying for a pre-matriculation test, we would have a film
> showing an IDF sniper firing a bullet at her head. If there had been a
> photographer near Jamal Jabaji from the Askar camp, we would see
> soldiers emerging from an armored jeep and aiming their weapons
> at the head of a child who threw stones at them ... it is certain that
> the IDF has killed and is killing children.[178]

THE FRAGMENTATION OF PALESTINE

> As far as I am aware, the imprisonment of a whole people is an
> unprecedented model of occupation – and it is being executed with
> frightening speed and efficiency.[179]
>   Tanya Reinhart, late Israeli academic and journalist

> We would like this to be an entity which is less than a state, and which
> will independently run the lives of the Palestinians under its authority.
> The borders of the State of Israel, during the permanent solution, will
> be beyond the lines which existed before the Six Day War.[180]
>   Israeli PM Yitzhak Rabin in 1995 on
>   Israel's view of the 'two state solution'

Israeli colonisation and a decades-long military occupation
have put immense pressure on Palestinian society in the OPT.
The economy has been reduced to a stunted, aid-dependent
shadow, a process that began long before the devastation of
the Second Intifada. Post-Oslo, average unemployment rose

by over 900 per cent between 1992 and 1996, while real per capita Gross National Product (GNP) fell by 37 per cent.[181]

That was nothing compared to the first two years of the Second Intifada, as the Palestinian economy experienced one of the deepest recessions in modern history, 'worse than the United States in the Great Depression or Argentina in 2001'.[182] By 2005, over 60 per cent of Palestinian households in the OPT were either in poverty or deep poverty, while the unemployment rate remained at just under 30 per cent in 2008.[183]

Collective punishment is routine, producing conditions designed to push Palestinians into leaving the land coveted by Israel. Israel's apartheid rule has territorially fragmented the OPT into an 'an archipelago of landlocked "sovereign zones"', subordinate Bantustans that Israeli architect Eyal Weizman describes as 'a permanently temporary Palestinian state'.[184]

Already by 2000, the West Bank had been fragmented into 227 separate enclaves, with only 17 per cent of the entire territory under full Palestinian control.[185] Around 88 per cent of these cantons were less than two square kilometres in size. The strategically placed colonies, the segregated roads, the Separation Barrier; Israel's iron grip on the OPT has only grown stronger with time.

If one looks at a blueprint of a planned prison, it appears as if the prisoners own the place. They have 95% of the territory: the living areas, the work areas, the exercise yard, the cafeteria, the visiting area. All the prison authorities have is 5%: the prison walls, the cell bars, the keys to the doors, some glass partitions. The prison authorities do not have to control 20–30% of the territory in order to control the inmates.[186]

Jeff Halper, Israeli Committee Against House Demolitions

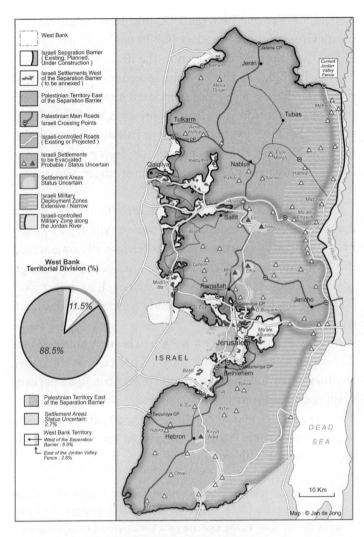

Map 5　Projection of Israel's West Bank Partition Plan – 2008

Source: Foundation for Middle East Peace.

Photograph 12   Qalandiya checkpoint near Ramallah, September 2005
(Andy Sims, htp://www.andysimsphotography.com).

PART II: CONCLUSION

Since 1948, Israel has maintained an apartheid regime over
the territory it controls, whether inside the internationally
recognised borders of the state or in the OPT since 1967
(Map 5). The nature of the apartheid regime in the OPT we
have just considered (land theft, colonies, separate roads, the
Wall, military brutality etc.) is manifestly not simply a case
of isolated human rights abuses, or even harsh restrictions in
the name of security. The checkpoints, settlements and raids
are all part of a systematic policy to consolidate and enforce
Israeli apartheid in the territories.

The nature of Israel's system of control varies, according
to the different dynamics on the ground and context-specific
objectives. Inside the OPT, where the Palestinians vastly

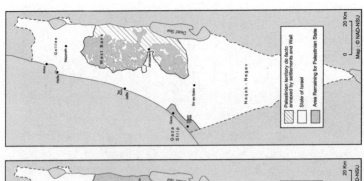

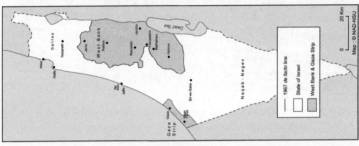

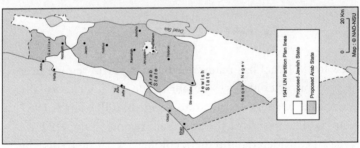

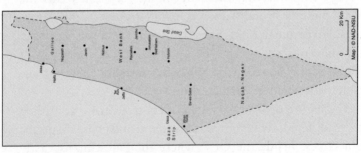

Map 6   Disappearing Palestine (PLO's Negotiations Affairs Department).

outnumber the settler population, a far more repressive regime is required to protect the colonisation process, compared to inside the Israeli state, where the Palestinian community is smaller and comparatively weaker.

Of course, around half of the entire Palestinian population as a whole are not ruled by Israel at all: they are the refugees and their descendents who were denationalised, expelled and forcibly kept out of their homeland by the first, dramatic acts of Israeli apartheid. Those who have remained are denied their basic freedoms as individuals and a people group, all in the name of the 'Jewish democratic' state.

Part III: Towards Inclusion and Peace – Resisting Israeli Apartheid

Resisting Israeli apartheid has always first and foremost been the work of the Palestinians who directly suffer the most. Families struggling over roadblocks with farm tools, villagers planting olive trees in groves surrounded by settlements, men waking at 4 am to queue at the checkpoints, activists living in fear of arrest or worse – ordinary people doing their best to live ordinary lives, confronting racism and colonial exclusion with defiance and dignity. But of course, defeating Israeli apartheid requires organised, committed and varied resistance strategies – locally and internationally.

Having introduced the concept of Israeli apartheid, how it came about and how it is being maintained, Part III of this book is intended to go a small way towards answering the question: 'What can we do about it?' Before discussing practical suggestions for international solidarity, however, we are going to have a brief look at a few organisations who are busy resisting Israeli apartheid where it matters the most: on the ground.

ON THE GROUND RESISTANCE

Adalah – the Legal Centre for Arab Minority Rights in Israel

Operating since 1996, Adalah ('justice' in Arabic) is at the forefront of legal efforts to challenge the system of Israeli apartheid. Independent, non-profit and non-sectarian, Adalah represents the struggle of the Palestinian population inside Israel for individual and collective equal rights in all areas of life.

Its team of lawyers go to Israeli courts to file petitions on a wide range of issues: land access, planning rights, police accountability, budget discrimination and more. In 2005 for example, Adalah submitted 20 new petitions and more than 35 follow-up cases.[1] In summary, Adalah:

- Brings cases before Israeli courts and various state authorities.
- Advocates for legislation that will ensure equal individual and collective rights for the Arab minority.
- Appeals to international institutions and forums in order to promote the rights of the Arab minority in particular, and human rights in general.
- Organises study days, seminars and workshops, and publishes reports on legal issues concerning the rights of the Arab minority in particular, and human rights in general.[2]

In recent years, Adalah has been at the centre of some high-profile struggles, such as the ongoing campaign to hold accountable the Israeli police officers responsible for the deaths of 13 Palestinian citizens of Israel, killed in October

2000.[3] Adalah is also heavily involved with challenging the discriminatory land policies of the Jewish National Fund through the courts.[4]

While investing a lot of effort in particular court cases, the group has also continued to advocate what it sees are the fundamental changes that need to take place in Israel to guarantee equality for both Jew and Palestinian. To that end, Adalah published its 'Democratic Constitution' document in 2007, a document that in calling for a state privileging no religion or race over another, was condemned by Zionist apologists as calling for the 'destruction of Israel'.[5]

The Association for the Defense of the Rights of the Internally Displaced in Israel (ADRID)

In the context of the increasingly significant peace talks between Israel and the PLO in the early 1990s, Palestinians inside Israel began to worry that negotiations towards a comprehensive settlement were neglecting the concerns of the Palestinian people living as second-class citizens in the Jewish state.

In 1992, community activists held a meeting in Nazareth and agreed on the formation of an initial committee that would work for the rights of the present absentees.[6] This led to the first nationwide conference in 1995, when representatives of almost 40 destroyed villages met together, turning the committee into ADRID.[7]

ADRID emerged as an umbrella organisation with three main aims: firstly, to promote the right of return of the 'present absentees' to their villages; secondly, to unite the various disparate efforts of Palestinians in Israel already working towards this goal; and thirdly, to raise the profile of the plight of internally displaced Palestinians domestically and internationally.[8]

Since then, the group has gone from strength to strength. In 1998, on the 50th anniversary of the Nakba, thousands of internal refugees went on a march to an abandoned village, while in 2000, 850 participants attended a rally in Nazareth.[9] Two years later ADRID was one of four international winners of 'The Body Shop Human Rights Award'.[10]

Uniting the various Arab institutions, political parties and religious bodies, ADRID's most celebrated annual event is the 'Return March' that takes place on Israeli Independence Day.[11] In 2008, on the state's 60th anniversary, thousands of Palestinian and Jewish citizens marched to the site of Safuriyya near Nazareth, a peaceful protest that ended with arrests and tear gas.[12] Throughout the year though, ADRID organises a variety of activities, and deserves much of the credit for the renewed steadfastness and determination of the Palestinian 'present absentees' to fight for their rights.

Israeli Committee Against House Demolitions (ICAHD)

For over a decade, ICAHD has been focusing on one very specific aspect of Israeli apartheid: home demolitions and the discriminatory planning system which they physically enforce.[13] Founded by Israeli sociologist professor Jeff Halper, the group's work ranges from rebuilding demolished Palestinian homes to campaigning domestically and internationally for Palestinian rights to be respected.

During the year, ICAHD organises 'working parties' of Jewish Israelis, Palestinians and international volunteers to help rebuild a demolished home. When possible, ICAHD members mobilise at the last minute to try and physically prevent the bulldozers from carrying out the demolition order. This 'hands on' experience with one aspect of Israeli apartheid has drawn ICAHD towards analysis and campaign work with a broader focus than just housing discrimination and demolitions.

ICAHD offer 'alternative' tours of East Jerusalem and the Occupied Palestinian Territories, in order to show people the 'facts on the ground'. For those who are not able to participate, ICAHD also provides information about the ever changing realities and policies to international diplomats and the media.

The organisation campaigns against the occupation, the violations of the Geneva Convention, and ultimately, the overall apartheid 'matrix of control' at the heart of Israeli colonisation efforts in the West Bank.[14] Halper's political analysis has been debate-shaping, highlighting Israel's exclusivist approach to the land, and providing a way to understand the evolving dynamic in the OPT.

In recent years, ICAHD has enjoyed successes and experienced challenges. It has chapters in the UK, USA and Norway, and in 2006, Halper was nominated for the Nobel Peace Prize for his work with the group.[15] But in 2008, ICAHD lost European Union funding, in what appeared to be a success for groups angry at ICAHD's role opposing Israeli apartheid.[16]

Popular Committees Against the Wall

In the last few years, the biggest threat facing thousands of Palestinians across the occupied West Bank has been the Separation Wall (see Part II). Communities have responded to this assault on their livelihoods by creating 'Popular Committees Against the Wall', grassroots, locally orientated initiatives intended to coordinate resistance to Israel's occupation policies.

Made up of those who are seen as trusted within the village the Committees also focus on Israeli land confiscation for settlements, a practice often closely tied up with the development of the Wall. There are Popular Committees all over the West Bank, including the Hebron and Bethlehem regions in the south, East Jerusalem, Ramallah and further up to the north.

In the village of Budrus, the first Committee was formed in the autumn months of 2003, quickly formulating rules for the organised protests against the Wall.[17] Other villages followed suit over the next couple of years, with perhaps the most famous example being Bil'in, in the Ramallah district.[18] Bil'in, whose story has often been covered by the international media, earned attention by forming a Popular Committee in early 2005, and organising regular non-violent demonstrations against the Wall.[19]

The Popular Committee in Bil'in has since organised international conferences held in the village. In 2008, the conference drew a crowd of over 300 delegates, including Palestinian Prime Minister Fayyad, Nobel Peace Prize winner Mairead Maguire and the European Parliament Vice-President.[20]

The relative success of the Committee, whose members have penned internationally published articles and pursued the legal path in the Israeli courts, has also made them a target for harassment by the Israeli soldiers.[21] While the Popular Committee in Bil'in has made the most headlines, Palestinians in dozens of affected villages have mobilised to protect their fields and olive groves, knowing that in many cases, they are fighting for their continued existence in the land.

Zochrot

While the remains of Palestinian villages, communities and mosques lie all over Israel, many Israelis today have no idea about the ethnic cleansing that took place in 1948, nor the 'hidden history' that lies beneath the surface of modern day Israeli cities, picnic parks and forests.

Zochrot, Hebrew for 'remembrance', is an organisation made up of Israelis concerned with raising awareness of the Nakba amongst their own people. As a member put it, 'most Israelis don't want to know this word [Nakba]' or even 'hear it'.[22] The group is not just simply about education and history; it is also very much about challenging Israeli apartheid as it stands today.[23]

One of Zochrot's activities is the placing of signs that commemorate Palestinian villages destroyed by Israel during the Nakba in the places where these communities once stood. This can bring them into conflict with Jewish Israelis who object to such 'political' actions, or even the Jewish National Fund itself. One year, Zochrot put stickers up around Tel Aviv, placing the words 'I almost forgot – today is Nakba Day' in speech bubbles coming out of people's mouths.[24]

Zochrot takes groups of Israelis to visit the remains of destroyed Palestinian villages, trips that can also include Palestinian refugees sharing about what village life used to be like.[25] On their website, Zochrot explain the hope behind their work, that by

> bringing the Nakba into Hebrew, the language spoken by the Jewish majority in Israel, we can make a qualitative change in the political discourse of this region. Acknowledging the past is the first step in taking responsibility for its consequences. This must include equal rights for all the peoples of this land, including the right of Palestinians to return to their homes.

INTERNATIONAL SOLIDARITY

While Palestinians and Israelis continue to resist apartheid on the ground, there is an indispensable role to be played by people around the world in realising a just peace in Palestine/Israel.[26] This small section will take a brief look at some of the possible strategies already being used by different groups around the world; there are many more ideas, and in every context, one tactic will be better than another.[27]

As with every movement, there can be disagreements about what strategies are the most effective or appropriate. The important point is that building a global campaign against Israeli apartheid that will really make a difference takes a whole variety of activities and strategies, by people from all walks of life: trade unions, religious groups, students, national politicians, students, town councillors, artists and many more besides.

At the back of this book there is a 'Resources' section where you will find a list of organisations and websites who work as part of the Palestine solidarity movement.

Boycotts

In several countries, there are ongoing efforts by various groups to institute Israeli apartheid-targeting boycotts. Some of these are 'consumer' boycotts, in other words, campaigns urging people not to buy products made in Israel, or sometimes, just the illegal settlements. Some campaigners approach supermarket chains and ask them to ensure that any produce they stock from Israel has not come from colonies in the OPT.

Other boycotts can be of a more institutional nature, whereby a trade union or organisation urges its members to stop cooperating professionally with their relevant Israeli counterparts. There is also a campaign focusing on a cultural and sporting boycott of Israel, seeking to encourage the same kind of isolation experienced by the apartheid regime in South Africa.

Divestment

Divestment means withdrawing an investment in Israeli companies or international companies that are profiting from doing business with apartheid. Although this could be done on an individual basis, it more commonly refers to the actions of a group – like a church denomination – that decides to sell its stock portfolio, or cancel some other kind of investment, in the offending company.

Campaigning for political sanctions

Sanctions are perhaps the most intense form of international pressure as they are enforced at the highest governmental levels. Broadly speaking, there are three kinds of sanctions: military, economic and diplomatic. Military sanctions include the cessation of arms sales to Israel, while economic pressure would mean cancelling preferential trade agreements that Israel currently enjoys with many individual nations, as well as collective blocs (like the European Union). Diplomatic sanctions means restricting or cutting official inter-government ties. For all of these, it is vital to lobby one's elected representative, raising the issue of Palestinian rights and demanding action be taken against the international law-breaking apartheid regime.

Protest and education

For all the progress made in recent years with regards to awareness of, and participation in, the fight for justice in

Palestine/Israel, there is still a lot more to be done. Protest marches, sit-ins, public lectures, film screenings, publicity stunts, subversive advertising, city twinning – there is a huge variety of creative options.

Supporting grassroots Palestinian and Israeli groups committed to resisting apartheid

Another excellent response to Israeli apartheid is to support the Israeli and Palestinian grassroots organisations that are committed to the struggle for justice. This could be in the form of direct financial giving, or perhaps by helping to raise awareness in your region or country of the work done by the group in question. Another way is to arrange a speaking event, or even a tour, so that representatives of these groups can come and share their experiences on the 'front lines' with international audiences.

Go there

Some people, from many different countries around the world, decide to actually visit Palestine/Israel, to see and understand the situation better, and to get involved with projects on the ground. This could be a short-term 'fact-finding' type trip or a longer term stay when there is time to invest personally in a particular initiative – such as a refugee camp community centre, environmental work, a group like ICAHD or a university. Of course, many go each year as pilgrims, and it is vital that 'Holy Land' tours include meetings with local Christian communities and exposure to the reality of life for Palestinians. While going there is not for everyone, seeing Israeli apartheid at first hand is a uniquely powerful experience, and those struggling against injustice on the ground welcome the solidarity.

TOWARD A DIFFERENT KIND OF FUTURE

In what is deliberately intended to be an introduction to a big subject, this book does not have room for detailed descriptions of what a 'solution' either should or could look like in Palestine/Israel. To some extent, the answer to the question about what the future must look like is contained by implication in this book's description of Israel's apartheid: a just, lasting peace for both peoples can surely only come about by removing the various elements of the apartheid regime.

It is important to remember that this is not about trying to go back in time, or trying to 'undo' things that cannot be undone. It is certainly not about wanting to make Jewish Israelis feel unwelcome in what is also their home. Put simply, the struggle against Israeli apartheid is about Palestinians having the same rights in the land as Jews do: all the rights they have been deprived of since Israel was built on the rubble of the Nakba.

When a permanent political settlement for the Israelis and Palestinians is discussed, the conversation often quickly turns to the 'two-state solution' and issues such as borders and Jerusalem – sensitive matters to be delicately negotiated. Most of this 'peace' talk is anything but, based on unawareness, or the deliberate concealing, of the reality of Israeli apartheid. It is incredible that diplomats and pundits can urge Palestinians to be more willing to 'compromise' as Israel continues its policies of colonisation and dispossession.

Peace for Israelis and Palestinians will not primarily emerge from the precise details of a geopolitical formula – the foundations of any such lasting, political settlement are human rights, dignity and justice. One of the biggest obstacles then is the persisting Zionist mindset – that informs practical policies – which sees Jews as having exclusive rights to the land. The Palestinian presence is tolerated, so long as the natives play by the rules.

As we have seen in this book, the result of this attitude towards the Palestinians is that even the most 'liberal' of Israel's leaders have maintained or strengthened the apartheid system, ensuring that the Palestinian people remain scattered, denationalised and dispossessed. At the same time, Palestinian resistance to Israeli apartheid has too often suffered from crucial strategic errors as well as failing to acknowledge or reach out to the deep-seated fears of Jewish Israelis shaped by the Nazi Holocaust and anti-semitism.

In Part II, brief mention was made of some important documents put together by Palestinian community leaders inside Israel in the last few years. One of them was the 'Haifa Declaration', a paper prepared by the Mada Al-Carmel centre, with an emphasis that reflected the main thrust of the other draft constitutions and publications. The Declaration stated:

> our vision ... is to create a democratic state founded on equality between the two national groups... [a solution that] would require a change in the constitutional structure and a change in the definition of the State of Israel from a Jewish state to a democratic state established on national and civil equality between the two national groups, and enshrining the principles of banning discrimination and of equality between all of its citizens and residents.[28]

Sadly, there are those who advocate a compromise with Israeli apartheid, rather than its dissolution, arguing for 'realistic' expectations. The strange aspect of this approach, even leaving aside the morality of what it means for Palestinians, is that it assumes a peaceful future for Palestinians and Israelis can be built on injustice and domination. In fact, it will only be through dismantling Israeli apartheid, and guaranteeing the collective and individual rights of all the peoples of Palestine/Israel, that the people of the region can realise the kind of peaceful tomorrow previous generations have been denied.

Frequently Asked Questions

Isn't singling out Israel for criticism anti-semitic?

Racism that targets Jews, like all forms of racism, must be condemned and resisted. In fact, it is precisely this opposition to racism that motivates the critique of how Israel treats the Palestinians. Sadly, there are some genuine anti-semites who wish to try and use the peace and justice movement in Palestine/Israel to gain a platform for their ignorant bigotism. But this does not mean that to struggle against Israeli apartheid is anti-semitic.

To complain that Israel is being 'singled out' is at best illogical, and at worst, a deliberate attempt to shield Israel from criticism (itself a form of 'singling out'). Furthermore, Israel has been exempted from sanction for breaking international legal norms, benefitting from generous aid and preferential trade agreements from the USA and EU while doing so.

For the Palestinians, Zionism has meant expulsion, exile and subjugation – so of course they will 'single out' Israel, as will those who are in sympathy and solidarity with them. You wouldn't hear a Tibetan activist being accused of 'singling out' China – so why should Palestinians or their supporters be treated any differently, just because it's Israel?

Criticising certain Israeli government policies is one thing. But surely demonising Israel, and denying its very right to exist as a Jewish state is anti-semitic?

'Criticise but don't demonise', the defenders of Israeli apartheid will urge, meaning that only they can define the boundaries of acceptable debate. Some pro-Israel advocates try to set limits when it comes to discussing Israel and accusing someone of 'demonising' Israel can be a very effective smear tactic. It discredits their opponent's viewpoint and motivations, and intimidates the undecided.

One of these 'taboo' subjects is the nature of Israel as a Jewish state. In fact, although 'anti-semitism' is often the charge levelled at critics, among Jewish Israelis there is also much disagreement about whether a state should be defined in ethno-religious terms. But ultimately, the question of Israel's 'right' to exist as a Jewish state is not simply a matter of debate and controversy. For the Palestinians, it is something far more fundamental:

> When you demand that Palestinians acknowledge the 'right' of Israel to exist as a Jewish state, you are asking them ... to acknowledge that it was and is morally right to do all the things that were and are necessary for the establishment of a Jewish state in Palestine, even though these necessary things include their own displacement, dispossession and disenfranchisement.[1]

To question the right of a state to exist at the expense of an entire group of people is not 'demonisation', and nor is it 'anti-semitic'. For Israel to be a Jewish state, the Palestinians must accept continued dispossession and second-class status in their own country, which is not a recipe for a lasting peace for either Palestinians or Jewish Israelis.

The English have England, and the French have France. Why deny the right of the Jews to a state of their own?

On the face of it this sounds quite reasonable, but only because of a confusion about the nature of the relationship between the Israeli state and Jews. For example, France is the state of the French, every French person is a citizen of France and all citizens of France are French.[2] Yet with Israel, the self-proclaimed state of all Jews worldwide, the same statement is impossible:

> Israel is the state of all the Jews; all Jewish persons are by definition citizens of Israel; and all citizens of Israel are ... Jews. The third part of the proposition is clearly empirically wrong; thus the assertion that Israel is as Jewish as France is French cannot be sustained.[3]

The analogy with Islamic states like Pakistan or Saudi Arabia is also a flawed one, even though both have Muslim majority populations and incorporate aspects of interpretations of Islamic law into the state institutions and legal framework. Yet while some states privilege one religion over another, no other country 'claims to be the sole global representative of the faith' or 'grants citizenship to people solely because of their religion (without regard to place of birth or residence)'.[4] Most importantly, the question 'Why deny the Jews to a state of their own?' is misleading, as it is not merely a hypothetical discussion. Israel has been established as a state for Jews the world over *at the expense* of the Palestinians.

Undeniably, you can find racism in Israeli society. But why don't you condemn the hate-preachers and racists in Palestinian society as well?

Of course, there are some Palestinians who hold to racist views, and this is entirely condemnable. Sometimes this can be specifically anti-Jewish racism, which is also unacceptable, even taking into account the fact that Palestinians continue to be occupied, dispossessed and killed by a state that deliberately identifies itself as Jewish, and claims to act in the name of Jews everywhere.

So while any kind of racism is to be opposed and challenged, there is an important distinction to be made. Some people are content to highlight the loud-mouthed bigots that can be found in both Israeli and Palestinian societies, blaming them for preventing the 'moderate' majority from reaching a peaceful agreement.

In reality, while there are individual racist Palestinians and Israelis (like any society), an enforced Jewish superiority is intrinsic to the very fabric of a Zionist state in the Middle East. As detailed in Parts I and II of this book, ethnic and religious exclusivity are written into Israeli laws, and expressed every time the bulldozer blade cuts into a Palestinian home. It goes much deeper than the reprehensible beliefs of a few 'extremists'.

Isn't Israel the only democracy in the Middle East?

Israel certainly has many elements of a thriving democracy: the Declaration of Independence includes a pledge of equality for all regardless of race or religion; Palestinians inside Israel have the vote; there is a diverse, varied media. These features and others seem to make a favourable comparison with Israel's neighbours very easy. But scratch beneath the surface, and another picture emerges.

To praise Israel as a democracy is to forget the occupation. For over 40 years, Palestinians living under Israel's military occupation have been denied their right to self-determination, as they watch Jewish Israelis colonise their land. Israelis refer to the Occupied Territories as Judea and Samaira, or 'the Territories', and include the area in official maps of 'Israel'. In which case, under Israel's control are 4 million Palestinians without voting rights or any semblance of dignity. When Palestinians in the Occupied Territories did vote in parliamentary elections – for a polity with no effective jurisdiction over its territory – Israel's response was to boycott the government.

Moreover, as we have seen in Part II, even for Palestinian citizens of Israel, there is profound, institutionalised discrimination on the basis that they are not Jewish – the same reason why Palestinian refugees cannot return home. It's beginning to look like a strange sort of 'democracy'. In fact, it was Avraham Burg, former Knesset speaker and Jewish Agency for Israel chairman, who made clear the stark choice facing Israelis: it is either 'Jewish racism or democracy' – you can't have both.[5]

State discrimination against ethnicities and religions, in whatever form, is to be condemned, and most of Israel's Middle East neighbours are dictatorial and repressive. However, Israel cannot be spared from critique simply because there are other examples of non-democratic governments. Time and time again, Israel's defenders seek to divert attention by pointing to other human rights issues.

In 2005, Israel actually withdrew from the Gaza Strip. But instead of concentrating on building up an economy and demonstrating a desire for peace, haven't Palestinians responded to this painful concession with rocket fire and terrorism?

With the bitter political infighting, the images of Israeli settlers being physically dragged away by their 'own' soldiers, and the fulsome international praise, many were convinced that Israel's 'disengagement' in the summer of 2005 was a genuine compromise made for the sake of the peace process. International politicians and media commentators marvelled at how Ariel Sharon had become the 'man of peace' Bush believed him to be.

But in reality, the whole thing was a televised PR stunt. Israel was under international pressure to make a 'painful compromise' in the name of peace, and withdrawing from Gaza also offered the chance to relieve the 'demographic' pressure of controlling 1.4 million Palestinians. Moreover, Israeli leaders had made it perfectly clear that the redeployment meant simultaneously strengthening illegal settlements in the West Bank. In other words, it was more land, fewer Arabs.

Then-PM Ariel Sharon's own advisor later told an Israeli newspaper that the aim had indeed been to freeze the peace process. He boasted, 'Sharon can tell the leaders of the settlers that he is evacuating 10,000 settlers and in the future he will be compelled to evacuate another 10,000, but he is strengthening the other 200,000, strengthening their hold in the soil.'[6] In the aftermath of the pull out, the Education Minister stressed frankly the importance of the 'window of opportunity' Israel had won itself to consolidate the major West Bank colonies.[7]

Sharon himself was also explicit about the strategy, telling the Knesset that 'whoever wishes to preserve the large Israeli settlement blocs under our control forever ... must support the Disengagement Plan'.[8] A couple of months before the disengagement, the PM told an audience that the withdrawal from Gaza was done 'in order to strengthen those [areas] with a high strategic value for us'.[9] Days later, Sharon confirmed how 'at the same time' as withdrawing from Gaza, Israel was focusing its efforts on areas like 'greater Jerusalem' and 'the settlement blocs'.[10]

But even putting aside the real motivation, the Israeli government also tried to claim that now there were no settlers or soldiers with a permanent base in the Strip, there was no occupation, and thus no Israeli responsibility. The Israeli human rights group, B'Tselem, demolished this pretence:

> The laws of occupation apply if a state has 'effective control' over the territory in question...The broad scope of Israeli control in the Gaza Strip, which exists despite the lack of a physical presence of IDF soldiers in the territory, creates *a reasonable basis for the assumption that this control amounts to 'effective control,'* such that the laws of occupation continue to apply. *Even if* Israel's control in the Gaza Strip does not amount to 'effective control' and the territory is not considered occupied, Israel still bears certain responsibilities under international humanitarian law. [emphasis added][11]

In fact, Israel retained control over the Strip's borders, air space and territorial waters, the population registry, export and import abilities, and crossings.[12] Moreover, the Israeli military continued to routinely conduct ground raids inside the Strip, using the airforce for assassinations, spying missions and collective punishment.

During 2006 alone, the IDF fired some 14,000 artillery shells into the Gaza Strip.[13] Many of those shells were fired as part of 'Operation Summer Rain', a wave of Israeli attacks following an operation at the end of June by Palestinian militants that led to the capture of an Israeli soldier. During July, B'Tselem reported that Israel killed 163 Palestinians in the Strip, almost half of whom 'were not taking part in the hostilities' when they were killed (including 36 minors).[14]

Since Hamas's success in the Palestinian Legislative Council elections of January 2006, Gaza had been totally isolated, subjected to an economically and socially devastating siege which Israel continues unrelentingly. In March 2008, Amnesty joined the likes of Christian Aid, Oxfam and Save the Children UK, to release a report describing the dire humanitarian conditions Israel had created for Palestinians in the Strip.

The report said that more than 1.1 million people, about 80 percent of Gaza's residents, are now dependent on food aid, as opposed to 63 percent in 2006, unemployment is close to 40 percent and close to 70 percent of the 110,000 workers employed in the private sector have lost their jobs. It also said that hospitals are suffering from power cuts of up to 12 hours a day, and the water and sewage systems were close to collapse, with 40–50 million liters of sewage pouring into the sea daily.[15]

The legacy of over 40 years under occupation, plus a continued siege and punitive military operations; it is disingenuous to point to the giant prison that is the impoverished Gaza Strip, and blame 'the rockets'. Indiscriminate attacks on Israeli civilians by Palestinian armed groups are deplorable, but to consider Palestinian violence in isolation means ignoring both Israel's open intentions for the Gaza 'withdrawal' as well as the collective punishment Israel has inflicted on Gaza's 1.4 million Palestinians ever since.

When the Palestinians voted in 2006, they chose Hamas, a Muslim fundamentalist terror group sworn to Israel's destruction. How can the Israelis be expected to feel like making concessions?

Hamas was formed in 1987, 20 years into Israel's military occupation, and at the start of the First Intifada. Some

Palestinians, paralleling regional trends, were disillusioned with leftist or secular parties, and looked for an alternative politics. Hamas's popular support has been typically connected to the buoyancy of the peace process. During the Oslo years, when hopes of progress were high, Hamas's popularity fell. During the brutal Israeli repression of the Second Intifada, however, support for a more militaristic, radical strategy increased.

Sometimes, Hamas is lumped together with al-Qaeda as part of a global Islamic jihad, despite the huge differences in origin, context, social base and aims. This clumsy analogy is often drawn for propaganda purposes, and sometimes made out of ignorance. In fact, Hamas has demonstrated a flexible approach to pragmatic politics similar to other parties and organisations. In the last few years, depending on circumstances, it has held to unilateral ceasefires and key leaders have even expressed a willingness to implicitly recognise Israel's existence as part of a genuine two-state solution.

That is not to say that there aren't individuals within the group who are more focused on a religious agenda than a political one, though unfortunately, the Israeli government has chosen to assassinate important Hamas moderates, only strengthening the hand of the hardliners. Some Hamas leaders and affiliated preachers have also been guilty of anti-semitic rhetoric, while others have noted the anti-semitism of the 1988 Charter. According to leading Hamas expert Khaled Hroub, however, this document has since 'become largely obsolete', while even at the time it was the work of one individual. This is not the only shift:

The vague idea of establishing an Islamic state in Palestine as mentioned in the early statements of the movement was quickly sidelined and surpassed... Hamas has developed, and is still developing, into a movement that is more and more preoccupied with current and immediate, and medium-term, goals.[16]

The reasons for the surge in support for Hamas at the ballot box in 2006 were nothing to do with an upswing in the number of Palestinians seeking an 'Islamic state'. Hamas had proven itself to be efficient in providing a number of vital services, such as health care and charitable support, in stark contrast to the corrupt Palestinian Authority. A vote for Hamas was also a rejection of the plans entertained by the international community, Israel and the Fatah-dominated PA, as well as a symbol of defiance after years of brutal Israeli repression.

People talk about the Palestinian refugees, but weren't a similar number of Jewish refugees kicked out of Arab countries and welcomed by Israel? Couldn't this be seen as a 'fair swap'?
The creation of the State of Israel led to two substantial population movements in the Middle East. Between 700,000 to 800,000 Palestinians fled or were expelled from their homes, and forbidden from returning by the new Jewish state, while from 1948 through to the 1970s, around 850,000 Jews left Arab countries, with the majority moving to Israel. But the rough equality in scale is just about the only similarity.

Israeli professor Yehouda Shenhav once wrote that 'any reasonable person' must acknowledge the analogy to be 'unfounded':

Palestinian refugees did not want to leave Palestine. Many Palestinian communities were destroyed in 1948, and some 700,000 Palestinians were expelled, or fled, from the borders of historic Palestine. Those who left did not do so of their own volition. In contrast, Jews from Arab lands came to this country under the initiative of the State of Israel and Jewish organizations. Some came of their own free will; others arrived against their will. Some lived comfortably and securely in Arab lands; others suffered from fear and oppression.[17]

Some prominent Israeli politicians who themselves come from Arab countries reject the 'refugee' label. Former Knesset speaker Yisrael Yeshayahu once said 'We are not refugees. [Some of us] came to this country before the state was born. We had messianic aspirations.' MK Ran Cohen, who emigrated from Iraq, made it clear: 'I came at the behest of Zionism, due to the pull that this land exerts, and due to the idea of redemption. Nobody is going to define me as a refugee.'[18]

As well as the fact that Jews in Arab countries were actively encouraged by the Zionist movement to move to Israel, there is another big problem with the 'swap' theory – timescale. Dr Philip Mendes points out how 'the Jewish exodus from Iraq and other Arab countries took place over many decades, before and after the Palestinian exodus' and 'there is no evidence that the Israeli leadership anticipated a so-called population exchange when they made their arguably harsh decision to prevent the return of Palestinian refugees'. Mendes also concludes his analysis by affirming that 'the two exoduses … should be considered separately'.[19]

But the 'swap' idea is anyway illogical. One refugee's right – in the case of the Palestinians, a right affirmed by UN resolutions – cannot be 'cancelled out' by another's misfortune. Furthermore, 'the Palestinians were not at all responsible for the expulsion of the Jews from Arab countries' – while 'the

Palestinian refugee problem was caused by the Zionist refusal to allow the Palestinians to return to their homes'.[20]

Given the historical and logical flaws, the only way this analogy can be so tempting for some is its propaganda value. The World Organization of Jews from Arab Countries (WOJAC), for example, claim on their website that their mission is simply 'to document the assets Jewish refugees lost as they fled Arab countries'. Professor Shenhav, however, describes how WOJAC 'was invented as a deterrent to block claims harboured by the Palestinian national movement, particularly claims related to compensation and the right of return'.[21]

Dismayingly, but perhaps unsurprisingly, the US House of Representatives was persuaded to pass a bill in April 2008 that not only equated Jewish and Palestinian refugees, but also urged 'the administration to raise the issue every time the issue of Palestinian refugees is brought up'.[22] *The Economist* magazine described the non-binding resolution as having 'doubtful value', as well as showing 'once more the power of the pro-Israel lobby in Washington'.[23]

Haven't the Arab countries used the Palestinian refugees as a political football, leaving them to rot in refugee camps?
There is no question that the Palestinian refugees have received often shockingly bad, discriminatory treatment in neighbouring Arab countries such as Jordan, Syria, Lebanon and even the Gulf States. But the question implies that these Arab countries, which themselves still suffer from an under-developed infrastructure and other significant socio-economic problems, should have simply granted citizenship to hundreds of thousands (now millions) of refugees. In Western Europe, many citizens baulk at the idea of granting asylum to a pro-

portionately much smaller percentage – and this in countries well-equipped to embrace new immigrants.

Many of the Palestinians displaced from their villages by Israel in 1948 were peasant farmers. Cut off from their land and everything they knew, they were not at all equipped to make a living in an alien country with a scarcity of jobs. Finally, it should be remembered that the reason why so many Palestinian families became, and remain, stateless refugees is because Israel has refused to allow their return, destroyed hundreds of their communities and confiscated their properties.

Hundreds of thousands of Jews came to live in Israel as survivors of the Holocaust and because there was nowhere else for them to go. How can you simply label them as racist colonisers?

To describe Israel in terms of apartheid is not to dehumanise Israelis. In fact, the struggle for a just peace in Palestine/Israel emerges from insisting on the humanity of both Palestinians and Israelis. It's true that thousands of Jews fled to first Mandate Palestine, and then to Israel, escaping persecution in Europe and Russia. The majority of Jewish Israelis today, moreover, have been born in the land that they have every right to call home.

Anti-Jewish persecution certainly helps to explain how Zionism emerged, but cannot justify, or detract from, the realities of Israeli apartheid. It's not about name-calling, or denying how after the Holocaust, many European Jews felt like there was nowhere else for them to go. It is about recognising that the Palestinians also have a profound and deeply rooted attachment to their country and the question, then, is whether or not they will share that land as equals.

At the same time as it is vital to respect and understand the impact and legacy of the Holocaust, it is also sadly necessary to refuse those who would manipulate and exploit Nazi crimes in order to justify the oppression of the Palestinians.

Why have the Palestinians continued to reject a compromise with Israel, from the very beginning of the state in 1948, to Arafat's 'No' at Camp David?

The myth of 'brave but peace-seeking' Israel always let down by violent, compromise-rejecting Arabs is powerful and enduring. Israel's defenders argue that if only the Palestinians had accepted partition in 1948, rather than seeking 'Israel's destruction', everything would have been different. Likewise, for the propaganda war of the Second Intifada, the Palestinians – and Arafat in particular – were said to have turned down a 'best ever' offer from Israel at Camp David, instead opting for violence.

Let's take a look at 1948 first. As we saw in Parts I and II, the real story of Israel's creation – the Nakba – is very different from the sanitised, Zionist narrative. When the UN proposed partition, Jews owned less than 7 per cent of the land, made up a third of the population – yet over half of the land of Palestine was assigned to the Jewish state. Moreover, even in its proposed borders, the Jewish state's population would be almost half Arab.

Ironically, while Palestinians are often accused of 'rejectionism', the Zionist leadership only accepted the idea of partition for tactical reasons. First Prime Minister Ben-Gurion described a 'partial Jewish state' as just the beginning: 'a powerful impetus in our historic efforts to redeem the land in its entirety.'[24] In a meeting of the Jewish leadership in 1938, Ben-Gurion shared his assumption that 'after we build up a strong force following the establishment of the state – we will abolish the partition of the country and we will expand to the whole Land of Israel.'[25]

It should come as no surprise that 'the fear of territorial displacement and dispossession was to be the chief motor of Arab antagonism to Zionism'.[26] Palestinian Arabs had seen the Jewish proportion of Palestine's population triple from around 10 per cent at the end of World War I, while the Zionist leadership in Palestine made no bones about their political aims. A question worth asking then, is whether you or I would simply accept the loss of our country, or if we too would be 'rejectionists'?

A similar question can be posed about events at the Camp David negotiations of 2000. Contrary to popular assumptions, 'Israel never offered the Palestinians 95 percent of the West Bank as reports indicated at the time'.[27] The 'generous offer' was just another incarnation of previous Israeli plans to annex huge swathes of the OPT, retaining major settlement blocs 'that effectively cut the West Bank into three sections with full Israeli control from Jerusalem to the Jordan River'.[28]

To question why the Palestinians have 'rejected' compromise is to look at the region's past and present from a particularly skewed perspective. Palestine has been wiped off the map, its land colonised and its people ethnically cleansed. Expecting those on the receiving end to be satisfied with the crumbs from the table is both unjust – and wishful thinking.

Glossary

Words in *italics* in the Glossary text have their own entry

Annapolis Conference
A one day conference for Israeli-Palestinian negotiations, hosted at a US Naval Academy in Annapolis, Maryland, on 27 November 2007. It was organised by the Bush administration, and attended by Israeli PM Ehud Olmert, Palestinian President Mahmoud Abbas, President George W. Bush and numerous other international diplomats.

Areas A, B, C
The *Oslo Accords* divided up the *OPT* into three kinds of administration. Area A is under full *Palestinian Authority* control (less than 3 per cent), Area B is under Palestinian civil control and Israeli security control (25 per cent), while Area C is under full Israeli control (72 per cent).

Camp David
A rural retreat for the US President and location for the Israeli-Palestinian peace talks brokered by Bill Clinton in 2000. The Camp David talks ended without a final agreement, with the Americans, the Israelis (led by PM Ehud Barak) and the Palestinians (led by Yasser Arafat) blaming each other for the failure to close a deal.

Dunam

A unit of land measurement in Palestine. 1 dunam = 1000 m²
or a quarter of an acre.

East Jerusalem – Occupied East Jerusalem

In 1967, Israel occupied the rest of Jerusalem, which since
1948 had been under Jordanian rule. Israel unilaterally
expanded the municipal boundaries of the city, and illegally
annexed East Jerusalem, a move that has not been recognised
internationally. East Jerusalem, like the *West Bank*, is
occupied territory.

Eretz Israel

The Hebrew term used to refer to the total area of the Biblical
'Promised Land' believed to have been given by God to the
Jewish people, including all of Palestine/Israel and parts of
neighbouring Arab countries.

Fatah

Founded in 1959 by Yasser Arafat and others, Fatah had
become the main political party in the *PLO* by the late 1960s.
Historically, Fatah has been happy to use both armed struggle
and negotiations as strategies in the Palestinian national
struggle. The current Palestinian President Mahmoud Abbas
is a long-standing Fatah member.

Galilee

A region in the north of Israel with the highest national
proportion of Palestinian citizens.

Gaza Strip

A small slice of territory bordering Israel, Egypt and the
Mediterranean Sea, and considered part of the *OPT*. The

Strip is home to around 1.4 million Palestinians, many of whom are registered refugees. In 2005, the Israeli government withdrew all settlers, and redeployed the army. In June 2007, after increasing tensions, *Hamas* overpowered its rival *Fatah* and secured political and security control over the Strip.

Green Line
Refers to the 1949 Armistice lines between Israel and the neighbouring countries. It effectively marks the division between territory accepted as Israel proper, and territory militarily occupied by Israel since 1967.

Hamas
Founded in the late 1980s during the First Intifada, a religious-nationalist liberation movement encompassing political activities, religious education, social and charitable services, and an armed wing targeting Israel. Considered a terrorist organisation by Israel and many in the international community due to its attacks on Israeli civilians, including the use of suicide bombings. An increase in popularity saw Hamas win the *Palestinian Legislative Council* elections in January 2006. A bitter rivalry with *Fatah* has often spilled over into violence.

Israel Defence Forces (IDF)
Israel's military, including ground, air and naval forces.

Jewish Agency (JA)
One of Israel's 'National Institutions', the JA became a kind of government-in-waiting for the Jewish community during the British Mandate in Palestine, before receiving responsibilities for immigration and settlement by the Israeli state.

Jewish National Fund (JNF)
Founded at the beginning of the twentieth century to buy land in Palestine for Jewish colonisation. After 1948, the JNF was incorporated into the Israeli state's system of land ownership, increasing its holdings with the 'abandoned' property of Palestinian refugees.

Knesset
The Israeli legislature, located in West Jerusalem. An elected politician is referred to as a Member of Knesset (MK).

Labor
Founded in the 1960s, a left-of-centre Israeli political party whose leaders have included Yitzhak Rabin, Shimon Peres and Ehud Barak.

Likud
One of the biggest Israeli political parties, and ideologically right wing. Famous leaders have included Prime Ministers Menachem Begin, Yitzhak Shamir, Binyamin Netanyahu and Ariel Sharon.

Nakba
Arabic for 'Catastrophe' and the term used by Palestinians to describe their ethnic cleansing and dispossession at the hands of the new Israeli state in 1948.

Negev
A desert region in the south of Israel, home to Bedouin Arabs.

Occupied Palestinian Territories (OPT)/Occupied Territories (OT)
Refers to the territories conquered by Israel in 1967, namely the *West Bank*, *Gaza Strip* and *East Jerusalem* (although Israel has unilaterally annexed the latter). The United Nations and the International Court of Justice use the term 'Occupied Palestinian Territories' (OPT), though they are often also described as simply the Occupied Territories.

Oslo Accords
Signed in 1993 by Israeli Prime Minister Yitzhak Rabin and *PLO* leader Yasser Arafat, the deal led to the creation of the *PNA* and was intended to start a process of incremental transfer of sovereignty to Palestinians in the *OPT*, and eventual statehood.

Oslo (Peace) Process
The Oslo (Peace) Process began with secret talks between Israel and the *PLO*, which led to the signing of the *Oslo Accords* in 1993. Since then, the Oslo Process has been used to describe the subsequent agreements and the general framework governing relations between Israel and the *PNA*.

Outposts
Unauthorised settler communities in the West Bank, 'illegal' in the sense that they are not officially sanctioned by the Israeli government. Often emerging from existing, authorised settlements, outposts have historically developed into fully fledged colonies.

Palestinian National Authority (PNA)/Palestinian Authority (PA)

Created out of the *Oslo Accords*, the PNA (sometimes just referred to as the PA) administers the parts of the *OPT* granted varying degrees of autonomy (see *Areas A, B, C*). The President is Mahmoud Abbas and the Prime Minister at the time of writing is Salam Fayyad. This latter role is contested by *Hamas*, who contend that Ismail Haniyeh is the democratically elected Prime Minister (the *Hamas* government was dismissed by Abbas in June 2007 as part of the *Hamas-Fatah* conflict).

Palestinian Legislative Council (PLC)

The elected legislature of the *PNA*, albeit with the same limits with regards to sovereignty. In January 2006, *Hamas* won a majority in the PLC elections.

Palestine Liberation Organisation (PLO)

Founded in 1964 to fight for the Palestinian national struggle, the PLO aimed for the creation of a single, democratic and secular state in Palestine/Israel. In 1988, the PLO recognised the State of Israel, and in 1993, the group signed the *Oslo Accords* with Israel. Until his death in 2004, Yasser Arafat was PLO Chairman, and was succeeded by Mahmoud Abbas.

The peace process

The general term used to describe official, high level negotiations between Israeli and Palestinian political leaders since the early 1990s (initially in the context of the *Oslo Process*). It is now a more general term to describe ongoing, international diplomatic efforts to resolve the conflict,

premised on the idea of dividing Palestine/Israel into one
Jewish state and one Palestinian state.

Present absentees/internally displaced Palestinians
Present absentees/internally displaced Palestinians are
internal refugees within the State of Israel who were declared
'absent' from their villages during the 1948 war and were
prevented from returning to their property. Around one in
four Palestinian citizens of Israel are internally displaced.

Separation Wall
The Separation Wall is the barrier being built by Israel in the
OPT since 2003, ostensibly as a security measure. In 2004,
the International Court of Justice ruled that the Wall is illegal
and should be removed. The Court also said that the term
'wall' was perfectly appropriate, since no one word perfectly
fits the combination of concrete wall, electric fences, gates,
trenches and military-only roads.

Settlements – colonies
Jewish communities established by the Israeli government
in the OPT since 1967, in contravention of international
law. Some settlers are religiously motivated, but others are
drawn by government financial incentives. The need to protect
settlements is a core principle behind Israeli apartheid policies
towards Palestinians in the West Bank.

West Bank
Territory that borders with Israel and Jordan, and under
Israeli military occupation since 1967. Home to around
2.5 million Palestinians (including East Jerusalem), and to
around 475,000 Israeli settlers living in illegal colonies. Major

cities include Ramallah, Bethlehem, Nablus, Hebron, Jenin and Jericho.

World Zionist Organization (WZO)
Beginning in 1897 at the First Zionist Congress, the WZO served as the main organisation coordinating Zionist efforts at creating a state in Palestine. It is also one of Israel's 'National Institutions', and has an official relationship with the State of Israel.

Zionism
A political movement that emerged in nineteenth-century Europe seeking to create a Jewish state, founded by Theodor Herzl. A response to anti-semitism, the Zionist movement soon rejected other geographical locations, and sought to realise the objective of Jewish statehood in Palestine.

Israeli Apartheid: A Timeline

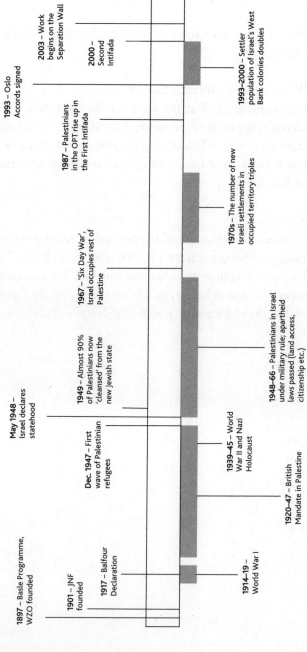

1897 – Basle Programme, WZO founded

1901 – JNF founded

1917 – Balfour Declaration

1914–19 – World War I

1920–47 – British Mandate in Palestine

1939–45 – World War II and Nazi Holocaust

Dec. 1947 – First wave of Palestinian refugees

May 1948 – Israel declares statehood

1948–66 – Palestinians in Israel under military rule; apartheid laws passed (land access, citizenship etc.)

1949 – Almost 90% of Palestinians now 'cleansed' from the new Jewish state

1967 – 'Six Day War', Israel occupies rest of Palestine

1970s – The number of new Israeli settlements in occupied territory triples

1987 – Palestinians in the OPT rise up in the First Intifada

1993 – Oslo Accords signed

1993–2000 – Settler population of Israel's West Bank colonies doubles

2000 – Second Intifada

2003 – Work begins on the Separation Wall

Resources

The author and publisher are not responsible for the content of websites.

NEWS

Al-Jazeera English (English version of the leading Arabic language news service): http://english.aljazeera.net

Alternative Information Centre: www.alternativenews.org

Antiwar.com (daily updated compilation of world news stories): www.antiwar.com

BBC News (latest worldwide news): http://news.bbc.co.uk

Guardian: www.guardian.co.uk/world

Ha'aretz (Israeli newspaper, regularly updated news): www.haaretz.com

International Middle East Media Centre (IMEMC): www.imemc.org

Jerusalem Post (Israeli newspaper, regularly updated news): www.jpost.com

Ma'an (Palestinian news agency): www.maannews.net/en

Palestine News Network (PNN): http://english.pnn.ps

Ynetnews.com (English site version of Israeli newspaper *Yediot Aharanot*): www.ynetnews.com

ANALYSIS

The Electronic Intifada: http://electronicintifada.net

Institute for Middle East Understanding (IMEU): www.imeu.net

Institute for Palestine Studies: www.palestine-studies.org

The Middle East Research and Information Project/Middle East Report: www.merip.org

MIFTAH (The Palestinian Initiative for the Promotion of Global Dialogue and Democracy): www.miftah.org

Le Monde Diplomatique: http://mondediplo.com

Palestine Chronicle: www.palestinechronicle.com

Palestine-Israel Journal: www.pij.org

Washington Report on Middle East Affairs: www.wrmea.com

INFORMATION (e.g. MAPS, STATISTICS)

Applied Research Institute of Jerusalem: www.arij.org

Foundation for Middle East Peace: www.fmep.org

Palestinian Academic Society for the Study of International Affairs (PASSIA): www.passia.org

PLO Negotiations Affairs Department: www.nad-plo.org

UN's Office for the Coordination of Humanitarian Affairs – Occupied Palestinian Territory: www.ochaopt.org

United Nations Relief and Works Agency for Palestine Refugees in the Near East (UNRWA): www.un.org/unrwa/english.html

HUMAN RIGHTS AND NGOs

Adalah – The Legal Centre for Arab Minority Rights in Israel: www.adalah.org/eng

ADDAMEER – Prisoner Support and Human Rights Association: www.addameer.org

Al-Haq: www.alhaq.org

Alternative Tourism Group: www.atg.ps

Amnesty International: www.amnesty.org

Amos Trust: www.amostrust.org

Anarchists Against the Wall: www.awalls.org

The Arab Association for Human Rights: www.arabhra.org

The Association for Civil Rights in Israel: www.acri.org.il/eng

Association for the Defence of the Rights of the Internally Displaced in Israel (ADRID)

The Association of Forty: www.assoc40.org

BADIL – Resource Centre for Palestinian Residency and Refugees' Rights: www.badil.org

Bimkom – Planners for Planning Rights: www.bimkom.org

Breaking the Silence: www.breakingthesilence.org.il

B'Tselem – The Israeli Information Centre for Human Rights in the Occupied Territories: www.btselem.org/English

Christian Aid: www.christian-aid.org.uk

Christian Peacemaker Teams: www.cpt.org/work/palestine

Combatants for Peace: www.combatantsforpeace.org

Ecumenical Accompaniment Programme in Palestine and Israel (EAPPI): www.eappi.org

Gisha – Legal Centre for Freedom of Movement: www.gisha.org

Gush-Shalom: www.gush-shalom.org

HaMoked – Centre for the Defence of the Individual: www.hamoked.org

Holy Land Trust: www.holylandtrust.org

Human Rights Watch: www.hrw.org

International Solidarity Movement (ISM): www.palsolidarity.org

Israeli Committee Against House Demolitions (ICAHD):
www.ichad.org/eng
Ittijah (Union of Arab Community-Based Associations):
www.ittijah.org
MachsomWatch: www.machsomwatch.org/en
Mada al-Carmel (Arab Center for Applied Social Research):
www.mada-research.org
Medical Aid for Palestinians: www.map-uk.org
Middle East Fellowship: www.middleeastfellowship.org
Mossawa Centre – The Advocacy Centre for Arab Citizens
in Israel: www.mossawacenter.org
Open Bethlehem: www.openbethlehem.org
Palestine Red Crescent Society: www.palestinercs.org
Palestinian Centre for Human Rights: www.pchrgaza.org
Palestinian Hydrology Group: www.phg.org
Physicians for Human Rights – Israel: www.phr.org.il/phr
Rabbis for Human Rights: http://rhr.israel.net
Sabeel – Ecumenical Liberation Theology Centre, Jerusalem:
www.sabeel.org
Ta'ayush – Arab-Jewish Partnership: www.taayush.org
War on Want: www.waronwant.org
Women in Black: www.womeninblack.org
Yesh-Gvul (There Is a Limit!): www.yeshgvul.org
Zochrot (Remembrance): www.zochrot.org

INTERNATIONAL SOLIDARITY AND CAMPAIGNING

Boycott Divestment Sanctions: http://bdsmovement.org
Palestinian Campaign for the Academic and Cultural Boycott
of Israel (PACBI): www.pacbi.org
Stop the Wall: www.stopthewall.org

UK

Al-Awda, The Palestine Right of Return – UK: www.al-awda.org.uk

Architects and Planners for Justice in Palestine: http://apjp.org

British Committee for the Universities for Palestine: www.bricup.org.uk

The Council for Arab-British Understanding (CAABU): www.caabu.org

Friends of Al-Aqsa: www.aqsa.org.uk

Friends of Bir Zeit University: www.fobzu.org

International Jewish Anti-Zionist Network: www.ijsn.net

Jews for Justice for Palestinians: www.jfjfp.org

Palestine Solidarity Campaign: www.palestinecampaign.org

Scottish Palestine Solidarity Campaign: www.scottishpsc.org.uk

Twinning with Palestine: www.twinningwithpalestine.net

Canada

Canada – Palestine Support Network: www.canpalnet.ca

Coalition Against Israeli Apartheid: www.caiaweb.org

Palestine House Educational and Cultural Centre: www.palestinehouse.com

Solidarity for Palestinian Human Rights: http://sphr.org

The Palestine Right to Return Group: www.al-awda.ca

Not In Our Name (NION): Jewish Voices Opposing Zionism: www.nion.ca

Students for Palestinian Rights: http://sfpr.uwaterloo.ca

USA

Adalah-NY, The Coalition for Justice in the Middle East: www.adalahny.org

Al-Awda, The Palestine Right to Return Coalition: www.
al-awda.org

Jewish Voice for Peace : www.jewishvoiceforpeace.org

The Palestine Freedom Project: www.palestinefreedom.org

The Palestine Solidarity Movement: www.palestinesolidarity
movement.org

Somerville Divestment Project: www.divestmentproject.org

Students for Justice in Palestine (various chapters at universities
nationwide), e.g. UC Berkeley http://calsjp.org

US Campaign to End the Israeli Occupation: www.endtheoc-
cupation.org

South Africa

End the Occupation – South Africa: www.endtheoccupation.
org.za

Palestine Solidarity Committee/South Africa: http://psc.org.za

Ireland

Ireland Palestine Solidarity Campaign: www.ipsc.ie

Australia

60 Years of Al-Nakba: www.1948.com.au

Coalition for Justice and Peace in Palestine: www.coalition-
forpalestine.org

The Australian Friends of Palestine: www.friendsofpalestine.
org.au

Australians for Justice and Peace in Palestine: http://ajpp.
wordpress.com

Australians for Palestine: www.australiansforpalestine.com

Notes

INTRODUCING ISRAELI APARTHEID

1. Mona N. Younis, *Liberation and Democratization*, Minneapolis, MN: University of Minnesota Press, 2000, p. 12.
2. 'Jabotinsky most popular street name in Israel', Ynetnews.com, 28 November 2007.
3. Nur Masalha, *Expulsion of the Palestinians*, Washington, DC: Institute for Palestine Studies, 2001, p. 28.
4. Avi Shlaim, *The Iron Wall*, New York: W.W. Norton, 2000, p. 13.
5. Office of the High Commissioner for Human Rights website, http://www.unhchr.ch/html/menu3/b/11.htm (last accessed 5 November 2008).
6. 'Rome Statute of the International Criminal Court', http://untreaty.un.org/cod/icc/statute/romefra.htm (last accessed 5 November 2008).
7. 'Israel must end the hatred now', *Observer*, 15 October 2000.
8. Leila Farsakh, 'Israel: an apartheid state?' *Le Monde Diplomatique*, November 2003.
9. *Ha'aretz*, 12 July 2008.
10. In an echo of Israeli land ownership laws, the Native Land Act of 1913 and the Native Trust and Land Act of 1936 designated 93 and 87 per cent of South African land respectively off-limits to native African acquisition. See John Quigley, *Palestine and Israel: A Challenge to Justice*, Durham, NC: Duke University Press, 1990, pp. 124–5.
11. Lindsay Bremner, 'Border/Skin', in Michael Sorkin (ed.), *Against the Wall*, New York: The New Press, 2005, pp. 122–37 (123).
12. Bremner, 'Border/Skin', p. 129.
13. Tanya Reinhart, 'The era of yellow territories', *Ha'aretz*, 27 May 1994.

14. Desmond Tutu, *Hope and Suffering*, London: Fount Paperbacks, 1984, pp. 94–5.

15. Bremner, 'Border/Skin', p. 127.

16. Uri Davis, *Apartheid Israel,* London: Zed Books, 2003, p. 84.

17. Lorenzo Veracini, *Israel and Settler Society*, London: Pluto Press, 2006, p. 18.

18. Farsakh, 'Israel: an apartheid state?'

19. Roselle Tekiner, 'The "Who is a Jew?" controversy in Israel: a product of political Zionism', in Roselle Tekiner, Samir Abed-Rabbo and Norton Mezvinsky (eds), *Anti-Zionism: Analytical Reflections*, Brattleboro, VT: Amana Books, 1989, pp. 62–89 (71).

20. Moshe Machover, 'Is it apartheid?' Jewish Voice for Peace website, 15 December 2004, http://www.jewishvoiceforpeace.org/publish/article_417.shtml (last accessed 5 November 2008).

21. 'History on the line: Joseph Massad and Benny Morris discuss the Middle East', in Joseph A. Massad, *The Persistence of the Palestinian Question*, Oxon: Routledge, 2006, pp. 154–65 (163).

22. Bremner, 'Border/Skin', p. 131.

23. Joel Peters, *Israel and Africa: The Problematic Friendship*, London: British Academic Press, 1992, p. 53.

24. N.A. Rose, *The Gentile Zionists: A Study in Anglo-Zionist Diplomacy, 1929–1939*, London: Routledge, 1973, p. 5; Richard P. Stevens, 'Smuts and Weizmann', *Journal of Palestine Studies*, Vol. 3, No. 1 (Autumn 1973).

25. A/RES/39/72.C, 'Policies of apartheid of the Government of South Africa', Adopted at the 99th plenary meeting, 13 December 1984.

26. *Guardian*, 6 February 2006.

27. 'Brothers in arms – Israel's secret pact with Pretoria', *Guardian*, 7 February 2006.

28. Cited in Benjamin M. Joseph, 'Separatism at the wrong time in history', in Tekiner et al. (eds), *Anti-Zionism*, pp. 136–52 (136).

29. 'Apartheid in the Holy Land', *Guardian*, 29 April 2002.

30. 'Occupied Gaza like apartheid South Africa, says UN report', *Guardian*, 23 February 2007; see for example 'COSATU open letter in support of CUPE Resolution on Israel', *MRZine*, 7 June 2006, and '"This is like apartheid": ANC veterans visit West Bank', *Independent*, 11 July 2008.

31. *Ha'aretz*, 21 February 2003; 'Why the BBC ducks the Palestinian story', *The Electronic Intifada*, 6 February 2004; 'Worlds apart', *Guardian*, 6 February 2006.

32. 'Israel risks apartheid-like struggle if two-state solution fails, says Olmert', *Guardian*, 30 November 2007; Meron Benvenisti, 'Bantustan plan for an apartheid Israel', *Guardian*, 26 April 2004; 'Ha'aretz editor slams Israel at U.N. conference', *JTA*, 30 August 2007; 'The war's seventh day', *Ha'aretz*, 3 March 2002.

33. 'Israel could become pariah state, warns report', *Associated Press*, 14 October 2004.

PART I: ISRAELI INDEPENDENCE, PALESTINIAN CATASTROPHE

1. Anton La Guardia, *Holy Land Unholy War*, London: John Murray Publishers, 2002, p. 188.

2. *Ha'aretz*, 9 January 2004.

3. La Guardia, *Holy Land Unholy War*, p. 7.

4. Justin McCarthy, *The Population of Palestine*, New York: Columbia University Press, 1990, p. 10.

5. Hussein Abu Hussein and Fiona McKay, *Access Denied*, London: Zed Books, 2003, p. 67.

6. Gershon Shafir, 'Zionism and colonialism', in Ilan Pappe (ed.), *The Israel/Palestine Question: A Reader*, Abingdon: Routledge, 2007, pp. 78–93 (83).

7. Abu Hussein and McKay, *Access Denied*, p. 67.

8. Charles D. Smith, *Palestine and the Arab-Israeli Conflict*, Fifth edn, Boston, MA: Bedford/St Martin's, 2004, p. 37.

9. Abu Hussein and McKay, *Access Denied*, p. 68; *ibid.*, p. 123.

10. La Guardia, *Holy Land Unholy War*, p. 77.

11. Smith, *Palestine and the Arab-Israeli Conflict*, p. 36.

12. Isaiah Friedman, *The Question of Palestine: British-Jewish-Arab Relations, 1914–1918*, New Brunswick, NJ: Transaction Publishers, 1992, p. 197.

13. See Stephen Sizer, *Christian Zionism*, Leicester: Inter-Varsity Press, 2004.

14. Avi Shlaim, *The Iron Wall*, New York: W. W. Norton, 2000, p. 7.

15. Tom Segev, *One Palestine, Complete*, London: Abacus, 2002, pp. 395–6.

16. Baylis Thomas, *How Israel Was Won: A Concise History of the Arab-Israeli Conflict*, Lanham, MD: Lexington Books, 1999, p. 25.

17. Nur Masalha, *Expulsion of the Palestinians*, Washington, DC: Institute for Palestine Studies, 2001, p. 62.

18. Segev, *One Palestine, Complete*, p. 110.

19. Maxime Rodinson, *Israel: A Colonial-Settler State?* New York: Pathfinder Press, 2001, p. 74.

20. Arthur Hertzberg, *The Zionist Idea*, Philadelphia, PA: The Jewish Publication Society, 1997, p. 245.

21. Hertzberg, *The Zionist Idea*, p. 222.

22. Masalha, *Expulsion of the Palestinians*, p. 6.

23. Michael Makovsky, *Churchill's Promised Land: Zionism and Statecraft*, New Haven, CT: Yale University Press, 2007, p. 156.

24. Edward W. Said, *The End of the Peace Process*, London: Granta Books, 2000, pp. 313–14.

25. Segev, *One Palestine, Complete*, p. 119.

26. Donald Neff, 'Truman overrode strong State Department warning against partitioning of Palestine in 1947', *Washington Report on Middle East Affairs*, September/October 1994, http://www.wrmea.com/backissues/0994/9409074.htm (last accessed 16 February 2009).

27. Segev, *One Palestine, Complete*, p. 405.

28. Masalha, *Expulsion of the Palestinians*, p. 37.

29. Benny Morris, 'Revisiting the Palestinian exodus of 1948', in Avi Shlaim (ed.), *The War for Palestine*, Cambridge: Cambridge University Press, pp. 37–59 (39).

30. *Ibid.*, p. 40.

31. *Ibid.*, p. 43.

32. Masalha, *Expulsion of the Palestinians*, p. 117.

33. Interview with Benny Morris, *Ha'aretz*, 9 January 2004.

34. La Guardia, *Holy Land Unholy War*, p. 188.

35. Masalha, *Expulsion of the Palestinians*, pp. 94–5.

36. Benny Morris, *The Birth of the Palestinian Refugee Problem Revisited*, Cambridge: Cambridge University Press, 2004, p. 131; Benny Morris, 'Yosef Weitz and the Transfer Committees, 1948–49', *Middle Eastern Studies* 22, No. 4, October 1986, p. 523. Cited in Masalha, *Expulsion of the Palestinians*, p. 182.

37. Morris, 'Revisiting the Palestinian exodus of 1948', p. 47.

38. Segev, *One Palestine, Complete*, p. 405; Morris, *The Birth of the Palestinian Refugee Problem*, p. 60.

39. Morris, *The Birth of the Palestinian Refugee Problem*, p. 50.

40. Segev, *One Palestine, Complete*, p. 404; Benny Morris, 'For the record', *Guardian*, 14 January 2004.

41. Morris, *The Birth of the Palestinian Refugee Problem*, p. 41.

42. Morris, 'Revisiting the Palestinian exodus of 1948', p. 43.

43. *Ibid.*, p. 44.

44. Smith, *Palestine and the Arab-Israeli Conflict*, pp. 189–90; also see Kathleen Christison, *Perceptions of Palestine*, Berkeley, CA: University of California Press, 2001, pp. 61–94.

45. Rashid Khalidi, 'The Palestinians and 1948: the underlying causes of failure', in Shlaim (ed.), *The War for Palestine*, pp. 12–36 (12).

46. Smith, *Palestine and the Arab-Israeli Conflict*, p. 185.

47. Walid Khalidi, 'Revisiting the UNGA Partition Resolution', in Ilan Pappe (ed.) *The Israel/Palestine Question: A Reader*, Second edn, Abingdon: Routledge, 2007, pp. 97–114 (102–3).

48. Derek Gregory, *The Colonial Present*, Malden, MA: Blackwell Publishing, 2004, p. 86; Walid Khalidi, 'Revisiting the UNGA Partition Resolution', p. 106.

49. For example, the Hebrew University's first Chancellor Judah Magnes and philosopher Martin Buber both advocated a binational solution.

50. Morris, *The Birth of the Palestinian Refugee Problem*, p. 33.
51. Avi Shlaim, 'The Debate about 1948', in Pappe (ed.), *The Israel/ Palestine Question*, pp. 139–60 (149).
52. 'Israel: the threat from within', *The New York Review of Books*, Vol. 51, No. 3, 26 February 2004.
53. Meron Benvenisti, *Sacred Landscape*, Berkeley, CA: University of California Press, 2002, p. 328.
54. Andrew Bell-Fialkoff, 'A brief history of ethnic cleansing', *Foreign Affairs*, Summer 1993.
55. Drazen Petrovic, 'Ethnic cleansing – an attempt at methodology', *European Journal of International Law*, Vol. 5, No.3, 1994, pp. 342–59.
56. Ilan Pappe, *The Ethnic Cleansing of Palestine*, Oxford: Oneworld Publications, 2007, p. 89.
57. Morris, 'Revisiting the Palestinian exodus of 1948', p. 49; Benvenisti, *Sacred Landscape*, p. 121.
58. Pappe, *The Ethnic Cleansing of Palestine*, p. 147.
59. *Ibid.*, p. 72, p. 138.
60. Morris, *The Birth of the Palestinian Refugee Problem*, p. 235.
61. Cited in *ibid.*, p. 257.
62. Shlaim, *The Iron Wall*, p. 31.
63. Morris, *The Birth of the Palestinian Refugee Problem*, p. 172.
64. *Ibid.*, p. 361.
65. Segev, *One Palestine, Complete*, p. 511.
66. Interview with Benny Morris, *Ha'aretz*, 9 January 2004; Mazin B. Qumsiyeh, *Sharing the Land of Canaan*, London: Pluto Books, 2004, p. 36.
67. Interview with Benny Morris, *Ha'aretz*, 9 January 2004.
68. Morris, *The Birth of the Palestinian Refugee Problem*, pp. 237–8.
69. Pappe, *The Ethnic Cleansing of Palestine*, p. 57.
70. Rosemary Sayigh, *The Palestinians: From Peasants to Revolutionaries*, London: Zed Books, 2007, p. 96.
71. Morris, *The Birth of the Palestinian Refugee Problem*, p. 469.
72. *Ibid.*, p. 428.
73. *Ibid.*, p. 429; Pappe, *The Ethnic Cleansing of Palestine*, p. 169.

74. 'The fall of an Arab town in 1948', Al Jazeera English website, 20 July 2008, http://english.aljazeera.net/focus/ 60yearsofdivision/2008/07/20087116188515832.html (last accessed 6 November 2008).

75. Pappe, *The Ethnic Cleansing of Palestine*, p. 169; Morris, *The Birth of the Palestinian Refugee Problem*, p. 433.

76. Gideon Levy, *Ha'aretz*, 2 June 2004.

77. Morris, *The Birth of the Palestinian Refugee Problem*, p. 222; *ibid.* p. 225.

78. Khalidi, 'The Palestinians and 1948: the underlying causes of failure', p. 13; Qumsiyeh, *Sharing the Land of Canaan*, p. 36.

79. Pappe, *The Ethnic Cleansing of Palestine*, p. 104.

80. Morris, *The Birth of the Palestinian Refugee Problem*, p. 138.

81. *Ibid.*, p. 265.

82. Smith, *Palestine and the Arab-Israeli Conflict*, p. 200.

83. Pappe, *The Ethnic Cleansing of Palestine*, p. 54.

84. Morris, 'Revisiting the Palestinian exodus of 1948', p. 38.

85. Morris, *The Birth of the Palestinian Refugee Problem*, p. 514.

86. *Ibid.*, p. 515.

87. *Ibid.*, p. 532; p. 527.

88. *Ibid.*, p. 517.

89. *Ibid.*, p. 528.

90. *Ibid.*, p. 529.

91. *Ibid.*, p. 513.

92. Shlaim, *The Iron Wall*, p. 82.

93. Benny Morris, *Israel's Border Wars, 1949–1956: Arab Infiltration, Israeli Retaliation, and the Countdown to the Suez War*, Oxford: Oxford University Press, 1993, p. 432.

94. Shlaim, *The Iron Wall*, p. 82.

95. John Quigley, *The Case for Palestine: An International Law Perspective*, Durham, NC: Duke University Press, 2005, p. 232.

96. Morris, *The Birth of the Palestinian Refugee Problem*, p. 589.

97. *Ibid.*, p. 313.

98. Abu Hussein and McKay, *Access Denied*, p. 5.

99. Qumsiyeh, *Sharing the Land of Canaan*, p. 34.

100. Smith, *Palestine and the Arab-Israeli Conflict*, p. 200; Sayigh, *The Palestinians: From Peasants to Revolutionaries*, p. 99.

101. Abu Hussein and McKay, *Access Denied*, p. 4.

102. Morris, *The Birth of the Palestinian Refugee Problem*, p. 369.

103. Mike Marqusee, 'The great catastrophe', *The Hindu*, 9 March 2008.

104. Benvenisti, *Sacred Landscape*, p. 164.

105. Morris, *The Birth of the Palestinian Refugee Problem*, p. 390.

106. *Ibid.*, p. 393.

107. Benvenisti, *Sacred Landscape*, p. 14.

108. *Ibid.*, p. 34.

109. 'Report of the Commissioner-General of the United Nations Relief and Works Agency for Palestine refugees in the Near East', General Assembly 22nd session, 30 June 1967.

110. Nur Masalha, 'The historical roots of the Palestinian refugee question', in Naseer Aruri (ed.), *Palestinian Refugees: The Right of Return*, London: Pluto Press, 2001, pp. 36–67 (61).

111. Smith, *Palestine and the Arab-Israeli Conflict*, p. 279.

112. 'Report of the Secretary-General under General Assembly Resolution 2252 (ES-V) and Security Council Resolution 237 (1967)', released September 1967.

113. Thomas, *How Israel Was Won*, p. 183.

114. 'Report of the Commissioner-General of the United Nations Relief and Works Agency for Palestine refugees in the Near East'.

115. Nur Masalha, *The Bible and Zionism*, London: Zed Books, 2007, p. 84.

116. Tom Segev, *1967: Israel, the War, and the Year that Transformed the Middle East*, London: Little, Brown, 2007, p. 407.

117. Uri Avnery, 'Crying wolf?' 15 March 2003, http://www.gush-shalom.org/archives/article236.html (last accessed 6 November 2008).

118. Human Rights Watch, 'Razing Rafah: mass home demolitions in the Gaza Strip', 2004, http://www.hrw.org/reports/2004/rafah1004/5.htm (last accessed 6 November 2008).

119. 'Report of the Secretary-General under General Assembly Resolution 2252 (ES-V) and Security Council Resolution 237 (1967)'.
120. Thomas, *How Israel Was Won*, p. 183.
121. 'Report of the Secretary-General under General Assembly Resolution 2252 (ES-V) and Security Council Resolution 237 (1967)'.
122. 'The ghost city of 1967', UNRWA website, http://www. un.org/unrwa/67commem/stories/GhostCity.html (last accessed 6 November 2008).
123. Avnery, 'Crying wolf?'
124. *Human Rights Watch*, 'Razing Rafah: mass home demolitions in the Gaza Strip'.

PART II: ISRAELI APARTHEID

1. Eliezer Schweid, 'Israel as a Zionist state', World Zionist Organization website, http://www.wzo.org.il/en/resources/view. asp?id=1365 (last accessed 29 October 2008).
2. Mazim B. Qumsiyeh, *Sharing the Land of Canaan*, London: Pluto Books, 2004, p. 96.
3. *New York Times*, 14 July1992.
4. Virginia Tilley, *The One-State Solution*, Michigan, MI: University of Michigan Press, 2005, p. 147; 'Nationality status in Israel is not linked to origin from, or residence in a territory, as is the norm in international law', UN Commission on Human Rights, 59th session, 15 June 2002.
5. 'So this Jew, Arab, Georgian and Samaritan go to court ...' *Ha'aretz*, 28 December 2003.
6. 'I am Israeli', Prof. Uzzi Ornan, YnetNews, 9 August 2008, http://www.ynet.co.il/english/Ext/Comp/ArticleLayout/ CdaArticlePrintPreview/1,2506,L-3592969,00.html (last accessed 6 November 2008).
7. http://www.knesset.gov.il/laws/special/eng/basic2_eng.htm (last accessed 6 November 2008).
8. 'Equality and destruction', *Jerusalem Post*, 3 March 2007.

9. In March 2007, the Prime Minister's Office said that the Shin Bet security services would 'thwart' even legal activities aimed at harming 'the Jewish and democratic character of the State of Israel'. *Ha'aretz*, 17 March 2007.

10. *Adalah* newsletter, Vol. 43, December 2007, http://www.adalah. org/newsletter/eng/dec07/dec07.html (last accessed 29 October 2008).

11. Cited in Uri Davis, *Apartheid Israel*, London: Zed Books, 2003, p. 226, n. 51.

12. Davis, *Apartheid Israel*, p. 70.

13. 'Analysis: what kind of aliya is best to ensure the survival of the Jewish people?' *Jerusalem Post*, 1 January 2007.

14. Jewish Agency (JA) website, http://www.jewishagency.org/ JewishAgency/English/Aliyah/Aliyah+Info/The+Law+of+Return (last accessed 16 February 2009); Davis, *Apartheid Israel*, p. 203.

15. JA website.

16. Charles D. Smith, *Palestine and the Arab-Israeli Conflict*, Fifth edn, Boston, MA: Bedford/St Martin's, p. 220.

17. *Ibid.*, p. 221.

18. Hussein Abu Hussein and Fiona McKay, *Access Denied*, London: Zed Books, p. 73.

19. John Quigley, *Palestine and Israel: A Challenge to Justice*, Durham, NC: Duke University Press, 1990, p. 108.

20. Ibid., p. 106.

21. Nur Masalha, 'Present absentees and indigenous resistance', in Nur Masalha (ed.), *Catastrophe Remembered: Palestine, Israel and the Internal Refugees*, London: Zed Books, 2005, pp. 23–55 (32).

22. Abu Hussein and McKay, *Access Denied*, p. 88.

23. Ian Lustick, *Arabs in the Jewish State*, Austin, TX: University of Texas Press, 1980, p. 276 n. 26, Quigley, *Palestine and Israel*, p. 109.

24. Lustick, *Arabs in the Jewish State*, p. 57.

25. *Ibid.*, p. 58.

26. Roselle Tekiner, 'The "Who is a Jew" controversy in Israel: a product of political Zionism', in Roselle Tekiner, Samir Abed-

Rabbo and Norton Mezvinsky (eds), *Anti-Zionism: Analytical Reflections*, Bratteleboro, VT: Amana Books, 1988, p. 71.

27. Davis, *Apartheid Israel*, p. 36.
28. *Ibid.*, p. 39.
29. *Ibid.*, p. 40.
30. Quigley, *Palestine and Israel*, p. 118.
31. Benvenisti, *Sacred Landscape*, pp. 176–7.
32. Abu Hussein and McKay, *Access Denied*, pp. 151–3.
33. Israel Land Administration (ILA) website, http://www.mmi.gov. il/Envelope/indexeng.asp?page=/static/eng/f_general.html (last accessed 6 November 2008).
34. Statement submitted by Habitat International Coalition and Adalah, UNCHR, 62nd session, 13 March – 21 April 2006, http://www.adalah.org/eng/intl06/un-i6-jnf.pdf (last accessed 29 October 2008). At the time of writing, there is an ongoing legal case, a petition filed by the Adalah legal centre, which centres on the JNF's discriminatory policies. Depending on the ruling, there could well be developments regarding the Israeli land regime, though it is unlikely that any substantive change will take place. See http://www.adalah.org/eng/jnf.php (last accessed 6 November 2008).
35. Abu Hussein and McKay, *Access Denied*, p. 148.
36. Cited in *ibid.*, p. 146.
37. Quigley, *Palestine and Israel*, p. 124.
38. Tekiner, 'The "Who is a Jew?" controversy in Israel', pp. 62–89 (70–1).
39. Davis, *Apartheid Israel*, p. 40; Abu Hussein and McKay, *Access Denied*, p. 154.
40. Abu Hussein and McKay, *Access Denied*, p. 191, *Adalah* newsletter, Vol. 42, November 2007, http://www.adalah.org/ newsletter/eng/nov07/8.php (last accessed 6 November 2008); Human Rights Watch, 'Off the map: land and housing rights violations in Israel's unrecognized Bedouin villages', March 2008, http://www.hrw.org/reports/2008/iopt0308/4.htm#_ Toc193705071 (last accessed 6 November 2008).
41. Tom Segev, *1949: The First Israelis*, New York: Henry Holt and Company, 1998, p. 67.

42. Lustick, *Arabs in the Jewish State*, p. 68.

43. Sandy Sufian and Mark LeVine (eds), *Reapproaching Borders: New Perspectives on the Study of Israel-Palestine*, Lanham, MD: Rowman & Littlefield Publishers Inc., 2007, p. 82.

44. *Ibid.*

45. *Ibid.*, p. 83.

46. Abu Hussein and McKay, *Access Denied*, p. 165.

47. 'Jewish Agency readies plan to foster a "Zionist majority"', *Ha'aretz*, 28 October 2002.

48. 'Jewish communities planned to "block Bedouin expansion"', *Ha'aretz*, 5 June 2004.

49. 'Battling against Israeli "apartheid"', BBC news online, 23 December 2004, http://news.bbc.co.uk/2/hi/middle_east/4111915.stm (last accessed 6 November 2008); 'For Israel's Arab citizens, isolation and exclusion', *Washington Post*, 20 December 2007, http://www.washingtonpost.com/wp-dyn/content/article/2007/12/19/AR2007121902681_pf.html (last accessed 6 November 2008).

50. Lustick, *Arabs in the Jewish State*, p. 192.

51. 'Only 4% of development budget allocated for Arab sector', YNetnews.com, 17 December 2007, http://www.ynet.co.il/english/Ext/Comp/ArticleLayout/CdaArticlePrintPreview/1,2506,L-3483728,00.html (last accessed 6 November 2008).

52. Jonathan Cook, *Blood and Religion*, London: Pluto Books, 2006, p. 123.

53. Gideon Levy, 'The threat of the "demographic threat"', *Ha'aretz*, 22 July 2007.

54. 'Arab birthrate drops for first time in years', *Ha'aretz*, 24 January 2005.

55. 'An alternative to child allowances', *Ha'aretz*, 2 March 2005.

56. 'Netanyahu: Israel's Arabs are the real demographic threat', *Ha'aretz*, 18 December 2003; 'Israel must remain Jewish', Ynetnews.com, 4 April 2005, http://www.ynetnews.com/Ext/Comp/ArticleLayout/CdaArticlePrintPreview/1,2506,L-3068007,00.html (last accessed 29 October 2008).

57. For example, see 'Boim: is Palestinian terror caused by a genetic defect?', *Ha'aretz*, 24 February 2004; 'The enemy within',

Ha'aretz, 30 August 2002; 'A "lite" plan for the enlightened voter', *Ha'aretz*, 21 March 2006; Oren Yiftachel, 'The shrinking space of citizenship: ethnocratic politics in Israel', *Middle East Report* 223, Summer 2002.

58. 'Legal violations of Arab minorities in Israel: a report on Israel's implementation of the International Convention on the Elimination of all Forms of Racial Discrimination', Adalah, March 1998, http://www.adalah.org/eng/publications/violations. htm (last accessed 28 October 2008). An Amnesty report in 2001 also found that 'various areas of Israeli law discriminate against Palestinians', 'Racism and the administration of justice', *Amnesty International*, 25 July 2001, http://www.amnesty.org/ en/library/asset/ACT40/020/2001/en/dom-ACT400202001en. pdf (last accessed 29 October 2008).

59. Adalah website, http://www.adalah.org/eng/famunif.php (last accessed 5 November 2008).

60. 'Forced displacement continues', Internal Displacement Monitoring Centre (IDMC), http://www.internal-displacement. org/8025708F004CE90B/(httpCountrySummaries)/893F40683 A0EF21EC12574BB002F8EF3?OpenDocument &count=10000 (last accessed 6 November 2008).

61. Adalah press release, 7 July 2008, http://www.adalah.org/eng/ pressreleases/pr.php?file=08_07_07 (last accessed 6 November 2008).

62. Abu Hussein and McKay, *Access Denied*, pp. 258–9; Adalah website, http://www.adalah.org/eng/backgroundlegalsystem.php (last accessed 6 November 2008).

63. Qumsiyeh, *Sharing the Land of Canaan*, p. 92; Association of Forty website, http://www.assoc40.org/Establishment.html (last accessed 6 November 2008).

64. Abu Hussein and McKay, *Access Denied*, p. 255.

65. Lustick, *Arabs in the Jewish State*, p. 51.

66. IDMC Country report for Israel, http://www.internal-displacement. org/idmc/website/countries.nsf/(httpEnvelopes)/F11200E8EC D83F71802570B8005A7276?OpenDocument (last accessed 5 November 2008).

67. The story of Kafr Bir'im and Iqrit is told in Nur Masalha's essay, 'Present absentees and indigenous resistance', in Masalha (ed.), *Catastrophe Remembered*, pp. 23–55 (36–41).

68. Abu Hussein and McKay, *Access Denied*, pp. 289–91.

69. Jeff Halper, 'The key to peace: dismantling the matrix of control', ICAHD website, http://www.icahd.org/eng/articles.asp?menu=6&submenu=3 (last accessed 6 November 2008).

70. Michael Ben-Yair, 'The war's seventh day', *Ha'aretz*, 3 March 2002.

71. Jad Isaac and Owen Powell, 'The transformation of the Palestinian environment', in Jamil Hilal (ed.), *Where Now for Palestine?* London: Zed Books, 2007, pp. 144–66 (152).

72. Quigley, *Palestine and Israel*, p. 174.

73. Eyal Weizman, *Hollow Land*, London: Verso, 2007, p. 116.

74. Amnesty International, 'Israel and the occupied territories, demolition and dispossession: the destruction of Palestinian homes', 1999.

75. Sara Roy, 'Decline and disfigurement: the Palestinian economy after Oslo', in Roane Carey (ed.), *The New Intifada*, London: Verso, 2001, pp. 91–109 (95).

76. Amnesty International, 1999.

77. Weizman, *Hollow Land*, p. 120.

78. 'Report on the situation of human rights in the Palestinian territories occupied since 1967', Mr Giorgio Giacomelli, Special Rapporteur, UN Commission on Human Rights, 56th session, 15 March 2000.

79. Amnesty International, 1999.

80. Weizman, *Hollow Land*, p. 81.

81. B'Tselem website, http://www.btselem.org/English/Settlements (last accessed 6 November 2008).

82. Foundation for Middle East Peace (FMEP).

83. Gershon Gorenburg, *The Accidental Empire*, New York: Henry Holt and Co., 2006, pp. 99, 101.

84. Quigley, *Palestine and Israel*, p. 174.

85. Weizman, *Hollow Land*, p. 46.

86. *Ibid.*, p. 92.

87. Marwan Bishara, *Palestine/Israel: Peace or Apartheid*, London: Zed Books, 2004, p. 135.

88. B'Tselem, 'Forbidden roads: the discriminatory West Bank road regime', August 2004.

89. Qumsiyeh, *Sharing the Land of Canaan*, p. 136.

90. Jeff Halper, *Obstacles to Peace*, Bethlehem: PalMap of GSE, 2004, p. 14.

91. B'Tselem, 'Forbidden roads: the discriminatory West Bank road regime'.

92. 'Israel's new road plans condemned as "apartheid"', *Observer*, 5 December 2004; 'Israel plans West Bank roads just for Palestinians', *Reuters*, 23 February 2006.

93. 'Israel accused of "road apartheid" in West Bank', *Guardian* citing *Maariv* newspaper, 20 October 2005.

94. 'High Court closes off use of major highway to Palestinians', *Ha'aretz*, 19 March 2008.

95. 'Palestinians fear two-tier road system', *New York Times*, 28 March 2008.

96. *Ha'aretz*, 2 December 2004.

97. *Ha'aretz*, 7 March 2002.

98. 'UN: No. of roadblocks in W. Bank up 7 percent from last Sept.', *Ha'aretz*, 4 May 2008.

99. OCHA Closure update, May 2008, http://domino.un.org/pdfs/GazaClosureUpdate0508.pdf (last accessed 28 October 2008).

100. *Ha'aretz*, 8 January 2001.

101. Anne Le More, 'Are "realities on the ground" compatible with the international state-building and development agenda?' in Michael Keating, Anne Le More and Robert Lowe (eds), *Aid, Diplomacy and Facts on the Ground*, London: Royal Institute of International Affairs, 2005, pp. 27–40 (30).

102. *Ibid*. p. 32.

103. Weizman, *Hollow Land*, p. 143; Roy, 'Decline and disfigurement: the Palestinian economy After Oslo', p. 100.

104. *Ha'aretz,* 24 September 2004.

105. IMEU Background briefing 4.13, 'What is Israel's separation wall or barrier?' http://imeu.net/news/article0080.shtml (last accessed 28 October 2008).

106. 'The barrier gate and permit regime four years on: humanitarian impact in the Northern West Bank', OCHA Special Focus, November 2007; OCHA Closure update, May 2008.

107. OCHA, 'The West Bank barrier', http://www.ochaopt. org/?module=displaystory&section_id=130&story_ id=1456&format=html (last accessed 28 October 2008).

108. 'Three Years later: the humanitarian impact of the barrier since the International Court of Justice opinion', OCHA Special Focus, July 2007.

109. 'West Bank barrier ruling: key points', BBC news online, 9 July 2004.

110. 'Red Cross slams Israel barrier', BBC news online, 18 February 2004.

111. Amnesty International, 'Israel/OT: Israel must immediately stop the construction of wall', 7 November 2003.

112. 'One thousand, two hundred and seventy-six people per week', Lawrence of Cyberia, 29 September 2007, http://lawrence ofcyberia.blogs.com/news/2007/09/one-thousand-tw.html (last accessed 6 November 2008).

113. 'Shin Bet: Palestinian truce main cause for reduced terror', Ha'aretz, 2 January 2006.

114. 'Address by Prime Minister Ariel Sharon to the Foreign Press Corps in Israel', Israel Ministry of Foreign Affairs, 11 January 2004.

115. 'Most settlements lie east of fence, most settlers west', Ha'aretz, 16 August 2007.

116. 'Touring Israel's barrier with its main designer', Washington Post, 7 August 2007.

117. Anita Vitullo, 'The long economic shadow of the wall', in Michael Sorkin (ed.), Against the Wall, New York: The New Press, 2005, pp. 100–21 (109).

118. Ibid., p. 112.

119. 'Letter from Jayyous', The Nation, 18 February 2004.

120. 'The barrier gate and permit regime four years on: humanitarian impact in the Northern West Bank', OCHA, 13 November 2007.

121. 'Israel's plans for cutting up Jerusalem', *The Economist*, 12 April 2006.

122. 'Settlers vie for East Jerusalem', *The Christian Science Monitor*, 12 December 2003.

123. Colin Chapman, *Whose Holy City?* Oxford: Lion Hudson, 2004, p. 148.

124. *Ibid.*, p. 156.

125. B'Tselem website, http://www.btselem.org/english/Jerusalem/ Discriminating_Policy.asp (last accessed 6 November 2008).

126. B'Tselem website, http://www.btselem.org/English/Jerusalem (last accessed 6 November 2008).

127. *Ibid.*

128. Amir Cheshin, Bill Hutman and Avi Melamed, *Separate and Unequal: The Inside Story of Israeli Rule in East Jerusalem*, Cambridge, MA: Harvard University Press, 2001, p. 38.

129. 'Israel remembers war, and its spoils', *New York Times*, 1 June 1992; also see 'A policy of discrimination: land expropriation, planning and building in East Jerusalem', B'Tselem, Extracts from a summary, May 1995; 'Committee approves construction of three new Jewish neighborhoods in East Jerusalem', *Ha'aretz*, 10 May 2007; 'PMO: "nothing decided" on new E. J'lem Jewish neighborhood', *Ha'aretz*, 20 December 2007.

130. Chapman, *Whose Holy City?* p. 156.

131. B'Tselem website, http://www.btselem.org/english/Jerusalem/ Revocation_Statistics.asp (last accessed 6 November 2008).

132. *The Economist*, 10 May 2007.

133. Chapman, *Whose Holy City?* p. 162.

134. B'Tselem website, http://www.btselem.org/english/Planning_and_ Building/East_Jerusalem_Statistics.asp (last accessed 6 November 2008).

135. Isaac and Powell, 'The transformation of the Palestinian environment', p. 149; Weizman, *Hollow Land*, p. 19.

136. *New Scientist*, 27 May 2004; Weizman, *Hollow Land*, p. 19.

137. FMEP website, http://www.fmep. org/settlement_info/stats_data/ miscellaneous/comparison_water_allocation.html (last accessed 6 November 2008).

138. FMEP website, http://www.fmep. org/reports/vol11/no3/03-sharon_speaks.html (last accessed 6 November 2008).

139. Bishara, *Palestine/Israel: Peace or Apartheid?* p. 138.

140. Amnesty International, 'Israel and the Occupied Territories: Mass detention in cruel, inhuman and degrading conditions', 23 May 2002.

141. B'Tselem website, http://www.btselem.org/english/Administrative_Detention/Occupied_Territories.asp (last accessed 6 November 2008).

142. Arab Media Watch website, http://www.arabmediawatch.com/amw/CountryBackgrounds/Palestine/PalestinianprisonersinIsraelijails/tabid/355/Default.aspx (last accessed 6 November 2008).

143. Halper, *Obstacle to Peace*, p. 13.

144. B'Tselem, 'Barred from contact: violation of the right to visit Palestinians held in Israeli prisons', September 2006, http://www.btselem.org/english/Publications/Summaries/200609_Barred_from_Contact.asp (last accessed 6 November 2008); 'ICRC urges Israel to allow prisoners family visits', *Reuters*, 26 May 2008.

145. B'Tselem website, http://www.btselem.org/english/Administrative_Detention/Index.asp (last accessed 6 November 2008).

146. B'Tselem website, http://www.btselem.org/english/Administrative_Detention/Israeli_Law.asp (last accessed 6 November 2008).

147. B'Tselem website, http://www.btselem.org/English/Administrative_Detention/Statistics.asp (last accessed 6 November 2008).

148. B'Tselem website, http://www.btselem.org/English/Torture/Index.asp (last accessed 6 November 2008).

149. *Ibid*.

150. Human Rights Watch, 'Torture worldwide', 27 April 2005, http://www.hrw.org/legacy/english/docs/2005/04/27/china10549.htm#ISRAEL (last accessed 16 February 2009).

151. 'Absolute prohibition: the torture and ill-treatment of Palestinian detainees', May 2007, Joint report with Hamoked, Center for the Defence of the Individual, http://www.btselem.org/English/Publications/Summaries/200705_Utterly_Forbidden.asp (last accessed 6 November 2008).

152. Amnesty International, 1999.

153. Halper, *Obstacles to Peace*, p. 31.

154. ICAHD website, http://www.icahd.org/eng/faq. asp?menu=9&submenu=1 (last accessed 6 November 2008).

155. B'Tselem website, http://www.btselem.org/english/Punitive_ Demolitions/Statistics.asp (last accessed 6 November 2008).

156. David Shearer and Anuschka Meyer, 'The dilemma of aid under occupation', in Michael Keating et al. (eds), *Aid, Diplomacy and Facts on the Ground*, pp. 165–76 (174).

157. ICAHD website, http://www.icahd.org/eng/faq. asp?menu=9&submenu=1 (last accessed 6 November 2008).

158. 'UN: 94% of W. Bank construction denied', *Associated Press*, 27 May 2008.

159. Amnesty International, 'Under the rubble: house demolition and destruction of land and property', 18 May 2004.

160. Benny Morris, *Righteous Victims*, New York: Vintage Books, 2001, p. 341.

161. B'Tselem website, http://www.btselem.org/english/statistics/first_ Intifada_Tables.asp (last accessed 6 November 2008).

162. Rosemary Radford Ruether and Herman J. Ruether, *The Wrath of Jonah*, Minneapolis, MN: Fortress Press, 2002, p. 115.

163. *Ha'aretz*, 30 June 2004; 'Diary', *London Review of Books*, 3 October 2002.

164. Derek Gregory, *The Colonial Present*, Oxford: Blackwell Publishing, 2004, p. 104.

165. Middle East Policy Council, http://www.mepc.org/resources/ mrates.asp (last accessed 6 November 2008).

166. 'UN report details West Bank wreckage', *Guardian*, 2 August 2002.

167. See 'Jenin: IDF military operations', *Human Rights Watch*, 2 May 2002; 'Shielded from scrutiny: IDF violations in Jenin and Nablus', *Amnesty International*, 4 November 2002; Rema Hammami, 'Interregnum: Palestine after Operation Defensive Shield', *Middle East Report*, 223, Summer 2002.

168. 'UNRWA: 45 homes razed in Rafah during Operation Rainbow', *Ha'aretz*, 26 May 2004; 'Operation Rainbow' on *The Electronic Intifada*, http://electronicintifada.net/bytopic/268.shtml (last accessed 6 November 2008).

169. Gideon Levy, 'Killing children is no longer a big deal', *Ha'aretz*, 19 October 2004.

170. 'Palestinian death toll reaches 202 as "Operation Summer Rains" extends into its tenth week', OCHA report, 24 August 2006.

171. Khalid Amayreh, 'Palestinian children killed by Israel', *Al Jazeera English*, 10 May 2004.

172. 'Palestinian doctors despair at rising toll of children shot dead by army snipers', *Guardian*, 20 May 2004.

173. *Guardian*, 6 September 2005.

174. 'Gaza girl death officer cleared', BBC news online, 15 October 2004; 'Israeli army under fire after killing girl', *The Christian Science Monitor*, 26 November 2004.

175. 'Gaza girl death officer cleared', BBC news online.

176. *Ha'aretz*, 14 December 2006.

177. Hammami, *Middle East Report*, 223.

178. Gideon Levy, 'Mohammed al-Dura lives on', *Ha'aretz*, 7 October 2007.

179. Tanya Reinhart, *The Road Map to Nowhere*, London: Verso, 2006, p. 157.

180. 'Address to the Knesset by Prime Minister Rabin on the Israel-Palestinian Interim Agreement', 5 October 1995, Israel Ministry of Foreign Affairs website (last accessed 16 February 2009).

181. Roy, 'Decline and disfigurement', p. 91; *ibid.*, p. 92.

182. 'Appendix II', in Keating et al., *Aid, Diplomacy and Facts on the Ground*, p. 219.

183. 'The Humanitarian Monitor', OCHA, No. 24, April 2008, http://www.ochaopt.org/documents/HM_Apr_2008.pdf (last accessed 6 November 2008).

184. Weizman, *Hollow Land*, p. 179.

185. Roy, 'Decline and disfigurement', p. 94.

186. Halper, *Obstacles to Peace*, p. 26.

PART III: TOWARDS INCLUSION AND PEACE – RESISTING ISRAELI APARTHEID

1. New Israel Fund website, http://www.nif.org/about/grantees/adalah.html (last accessed 5 November 2008).

2. Adalah website, http://www.adalah.org/eng/about.php (last accessed 5 November 2008).

3. Adalah website, http://www.adalah.org/eng/october2000.php (last accessed 5 November 2008).

4. Adalah website, http://www.adalah.org/eng/jnf.php (last accessed 5 November 2008).

5. Adalah website, http://www.adalah.org/eng/democratic_constitution-e.pdf (last accessed 5 November 2008).

6. Nur Masalha, 'Present absentees and indigenous resistance', in Nur Masalha (ed.), *Catastrophe Remembered: Palestine, Israel and the Internal Refugees*, London: Zed Books, 2005, pp. 23–55 (42).

7. *Ibid.*, p. 43.

8. *Ibid.*, p. 42.

9. *Ibid.*, p. 45.

10. BADIL Press release, 30 October 2002, http://www.badil.org/Publications/Press/2002/press276–02.htm (last accessed 5 November 2008).

11. Nur Masalha, 'Present absentees and indigenous resistance', p. 45.

12. Ben White, 'Israel's alternative independence day', *New Statesman* online, 9 May 2008, http://www.newstatesman.com/middle-east/2008/05/israel-palestinian-march-arab (last accessed 5 November 2008).

13. ICAHD website, http://www.icahd.org/eng (last accessed 5 November 2008).

14. Jeff Halper, 'The key to peace: dismantling the matrix of control', http://www.icahd.org/eng/articles.asp?menu=6&submenu=3 (last accessed 5 November 2008).

15. News release, 15 February 2006, American Friends Service Committee website http://www.afsc.org/ht/display/ContentDetails/i/5292/pid/449 (last accessed 5 November 2008).

16. 'European Union drops ICAHD funding', *European Tribune*, 8 September 2008, http://www.eurotrib.com/?op=displaystory;sid=2008/9/8/155932/5994 (last accessed 5 November 2008).

17. 'Letter from Budrus', *The Nation*, 28 May 2004, http://www. thenation.com/doc/20040614/sorkin (last accessed 5 November 2008).

18. See, for example Aboud village, where the Committee was formed in 2005, http://www.leicester-holyland.org.uk/18th%20%20No vember%202005.htm (last accessed 5 November 2008).

19. Bil'in website, http://www.bilin-village.org/english/discover-bilin/ (last accessed 5 November 2008).

20. Official coverage on Bil'in's website, http://www.bilin-village.org/ english/conferences/conference2008/ (last accessed 5 November 2008).

21. 'Help us stop Israel's wall peacefully', Mohammed Khatib, *International Herald Tribune*, 12 July 2005, http://www.iht. com/articles/2005/07/11/opinion/edkhatib.php (last accessed 5 November 2008); 'Israel told to halt barrier work', BBC news online, 29 February 2004, http://news.bbc.co.uk/2/hi/ middle_east/3520115.stm (last accessed 5 November 2008); For example, 'Crackdown on non violent resistance', 17 June 2005, http://www.kibush.co.il/show_file.asp?num=4650 (last accessed 5 November 2008).

22. 'Norma Musih, Zochrot and the Nakba', *Washington Report on Middle East Affairs*, May–June 2007, http://www.wrmea. com/archives/May-June_2007/0705025.html (last accessed 5 November 2008).

23. Zochrot website, http://www.zochrot.org/index.php?lang=english (last accessed 5 November 2008).

24. 'Norma Musih, Zochrot and the Nakba', *Washington Report on Middle East Affairs*.

25. Jacob Pace, 'Ethnic cleansing 101: the case of Lifta Village', *The Electronic Intifada*, 2 March 2005, http://electronicintifada. net/v2/article3652.shtml (last accessed 5 November 2008).

26. For a decent overview, see BADIL's *al-Majdal Quarterly*, No. 38, Summer 2008, http://www.badil.org/al-majdal/2008/summer/ majdal38.pdf (last accessed 5 November 2008).

27. The 'Boycott Divestment Sanctions' website is a great resource: http://bdsmovement.org (last accessed 5 November 2008).

28. Mada al-Carmel, The Haifa Declaration, 2007, http://www.mada-research.org/archive/haifaenglish.pdf (last accessed 6 November 2008).

FREQUENTLY ASKED QUESTIONS

1. 'Eggs fail to recognize omelette's right to exist', *Lawrence of Cyberia*, 6 March 2007, http://lawrenceofcyberia.blogs.com/news/2007/03/eggs_fail_to_re.html (last accessed 5 November 2008).

2. *The New York Review of Books*, Vol. 50, No. 19, 4 December 2003.

3. Sharif Elmusa, 'Searching for a solution', in Jamil Hilal (ed.), *Where Now for Palestine?* London: Zed Books, 2007, pp. 211–32 (223).

4. 'Memories of a promised land', *New Humanist*, Vol. 123, Issue 3, May/June 2008.

5. 'The end of Zionism', *Guardian*, 15 September 2003.

6. *Ha'aretz*, 10 November 2005.

7. *Ha'aretz*, 6 September 2005.

8. Prime Minister Ariel Sharon's Speech at the Knesset, 22 April 2004, http://www.pmo.gov.il/PMOEng/Archive/Speeches/2004/04/Speeches7887.htm (last accessed 5 November 2008).

9. 'Israel will strengthen strategic bases after Gaza pullout: PM', *AFP*, 16 June 2005.

10. Prime Minister Ariel Sharon's Speech at the Jewish Agency Assembly, 28 June 2005, http://www.pmo.gov.il/PMOEng/Archive/Speeches/2005/06/speech2806.htm (last accessed 5 November 2008).

11. B'Tselem website http://www.btselem.org/english/Gaza_Strip/Israels_obligations.asp (last accessed 5 November 2008).

12. B'Tselem website http://www.btselem.org/english/Gaza_Strip/Gaza_Status.asp (last accessed 5 November 2008).

13. 'Israeli-Palestinian fatalities since 2000', *OCHA Special Focus*, 31 August 2007.

14. 'Almost half the fatalities in the Gaza Strip in July were civilians not taking part in the hostilities', *B'Tselem*, 3 August 2006.

15. 'Study: Gaza humanitarian situation worst since 1967', *The Associated Press*, 6 March 2008.

16. Khaled Hroub, *Hamas: A Beginner's Guide*, London: Pluto Press, 2006, pp. 20–1.

17. *Ha'aretz*, 15 August 2003.

18. *Ibid.*

19. Dr Philip Mendes, 'The forgotten refugees: the causes of the post-1948 Jewish exodus from Arab countries', Australian Association of Jewish Studies 14th Annual Conference, March 2002.

20. *The Magnes Zionist*, 6 November 2007, http://themagneszionist. blogspot.com/2007/11/forgotten-refugees-jewish-refugees-from. html (last accessed 5 November 2008).

21. *Ha'aretz*, 15 August 2003.

22. 'House equates Jewish, Palestinian refugees', *The Jewish Week*, 2 April 2008.

23. *The Economist*, 10 April 2008.

24. Tom Segev, *One Palestine, Complete*, London: Abacus, 2002, p. 403.

25. Nur Masalha, *Expulsion of the Palestinians*, Washington, DC: The Institute for Palestine Studies, 2001, p. 107.

26. Benny Morris, *Righteous Victims*, New York: Vintage Books, 2001, p. 37.

27. Charles D. Smith, *Palestine and the Arab-Israeli Conflict*, Boston, MA: Bedford/St. Martin's, 2004, pp. 498–500.

28. *Ibid.*, p. 494.

Select Bibliography

Abu Hussein, Hussein and Fiona McKay (2003) *Access Denied* (London: Zed Books).

Amnesty International (1999) 'Israel and the Occupied Territories, demolition and dispossession: the destruction of Palestinian homes'.

—— (2001) 'Racism and the administration of justice'.

—— (2002a) 'Israel and the Occupied Territories: mass detention in cruel, inhuman and degrading conditions'.

—— (2002b) 'Shielded from scrutiny: IDF violations in Jenin and Nablus'.

—— (2003) 'Israel/OT: Israel must immediately stop the construction of wall'.

—— (2004a) 'Under the rubble: house demolition and destruction of land and property'.

—— (2004b) 'Israel/Occupied Territories: killing of children must be investigated'.

Baroud, Ramzy (2006) *The Second Palestinian Intifada* (London: Pluto Press).

Benvenisti, Meron (2002) *Sacred Landscape* (Berkeley, CA: University of California Press).

Bishara, Marwan (2004) *Palestine/Israel: Peace or Apartheid* (London: Zed Books).

B'Tselem and Hamoked (2007) 'Absolute prohibition: the torture and ill-treatment of Palestinian detainees'.

Bremner, Lindsay (2005) 'Border/Skin', in Michael Sorkin (ed.), *Against the Wall* (New York: The New Press) pp. 122–37.

Chapman, Colin (2004) *Whose Holy City?* (Oxford: Lion Hudson).

Cheshin, Amir, Bill Hutman and Avi Melamed (2001) *Separate and Unequal: The Inside Story of Israeli Rule in East Jerusalem* (Cambridge, MA: Harvard University Press).

Christison, Kathleen (2001) *Perceptions of Palestine* (Berkeley, CA: University of California Press).

Cook, Jonathan (2006) *Blood and Religion* (London: Pluto Books).

Davis, Uri (2003) *Apartheid Israel* (London: Zed Books).

Elmusa, Sharif (2007) 'Searching for a solution', in Jamil Hilal (ed.), *Where Now for Palestine?* (London: Zed Books) pp. 211–32.

Farsoun, Samih K. and Naseer H. Aruri (2006) *Palestine and the Palestinians* (Boulder, CO: Westview Press).

Finkelstein, Norman G. (1995) *Image and Reality of the Israel-Palestine Conflict* (London: Verso).

Friedman, Isaiah (1992) *The Question of Palestine: British-Jewish-Arab Relations, 1914–1918* (London: Transaction Publishers).

Garaudy, Roger (1977) 'Religious and historical pretexts of Zionism', *Journal of Palestine Studies*, Vol. 6, No. 2, pp. 41–52.

Glaser, Daryl (2003) 'Zionism and apartheid: a moral comparison', *Ethnic and Racial Studies*, Vol. 26, Issue 3, pp. 403–21.

Gorenburg, Gershon (2006) *The Accidental Empire* (New York: Times Books/Henry Holt and Co.).

Gregory, Derek (2004) *The Colonial Present* (Malden, MA: Blackwell Publishing).

Halper, Jeff (2004) *Obstacles to Peace* (Bethlehem: PalMap of GSE).

Hammami, Rema (2002) 'Interregnum: Palestine after Operation Defensive Shield', *Middle East Report*, No. 223, pp. 18–27.

Hertzberg, Arthur (ed.) (1997) *The Zionist Idea* (Philadelphia, PA: The Jewish Publication Society).

Hirst, David (2002) *The Gun and the Olive Branch* (London: Faber and Faber).

Hroub, Khaled (2006) *Hamas: A Beginner's Guide* (London: Pluto Press).

Human Rights Watch (2002) 'Jenin: IDF military operations'.

—— (2004) 'Razing Rafah: mass home demolitions in the Gaza Strip'.

—— (2005) 'Torture worldwide'.

Hunter, Jane (1987) *Israeli Foreign Policy: South Africa and Central America* (Boston, MA: South End Press).

Isaac, Jad and Owen Powell (2007) 'The transformation of the Palestinian environment', in Jamil Hilal (ed.), *Where Now for Palestine?* (London: Zed Books) pp. 144–66.

Joseph, Benjamin M. (1988) 'Separatism at the wrong time in history', in Roselle Tekiner, Samir Abed-Rabbo and Norton Mezvinsky (eds), *Anti-Zionism: Analytical Reflections* (Brattleboro, VT: Amana Books) pp. 136–52.

Khalidi, Rashid (2007) 'The Palestinians and 1948: the underlying causes of failure', in Eugene L. Rogan and Avi Shlaim (eds), *The War for Palestine* (Cambridge: Cambridge University Press) pp. 12–36.

Khalidi, Walid (2007) 'Revisiting the UNGA Partition Resolution', in Ilan Pappe (ed.), *The Israel/Palestine Question: A Reader* (Abingdon: Routledge) pp. 97–114.

Kovel, Joel (2007) *Overcoming Zionism* (London: Pluto Press).

Kimmerling, Baruch (2006) *Politicide* (London: Verso).

La Guardia, Anton (2002) *Holy Land Unholy War* (London: John Murray Publishers).

Le More, Anne (2005) 'Are "realities on the ground" compatible with the international state-building and development agenda?' in Michael Keating, Anne Le More and Robert Lowe (eds), *Aid, Diplomacy and Facts on the Ground* (London: Royal Institute of International Affairs) pp. 27–40.

Lentin, Ronit (ed.) (2008) *Thinking Palestine* (London: Zed Books).

Lustick, Ian (1980) *Arabs in the Jewish State* (Austin, TX: University of Texas Press).

Makdisi, Saree (2008) *Palestine Inside Out: An Everyday Occupation* (New York: W.W. Norton).

Masalha, Nur (2001a) *Expulsion of the Palestinians* (Washington, DC: Institute for Palestine Studies).

—— (2001) 'The historical roots of the Palestinian refugee question', in Naseer Aruri (ed.), *Palestinian Refugees: The Right of Return* (London: Pluto Press) pp. 36–67.

—— (2007) *The Bible and Zionism* (London: Zed Books).

—— (ed.) (2005) *Catastrophe Remembered: Palestine, Israel and the Internal Refugees* (London: Zed Books).

Massad, Joseph A. (2006) *The Persistence of the Palestinian Question* (Oxon: Routledge) pp. 154–65.

McCarthy, Justin (1990) *The Population of Palestine: Population History and Statistics of the Late Ottoman Period and the Mandate* (New York: Columbia University Press).

Morris, Benny (1993) *Israel's Border Wars, 1949–1956: Arab Infiltration, Israeli Retaliation, and the Countdown to the Suez War* (Oxford: Oxford University Press).

—— (2001) *Righteous Victims* (New York: Vintage Books).

—— (2004) *The Birth of the Palestinian Refugee Problem Revisited* (Cambridge: Cambridge University Press).

—— (2007) 'Revisiting the Palestinian exodus of 1948', in Eugene L. Rogan and Avi Shlaim (eds), *The War for Palestine* (Cambridge: Cambridge University Press) pp. 37–59.

Nathan, Susan (2005) *The Other Side of Israel* (London: HarperCollins).

Nazzal, Nafez (1974) 'The Zionist Occupation of Western Galilee, 1948', *Journal of Palestine Studies*, Vol. 3, No. 3, pp. 58–76.

Neslen, Arthur (2006) *Occupied Minds* (London: Pluto Press).

Pappe, Ilan (2007) *The Ethnic Cleansing of Palestine* (Oxford: Oneworld Publications).

Peters, Joel (1992) *Israel and Africa: The Problematic Friendship* (London: British Academic Press).

Piterberg, Gabriel (2008) *The Returns of Zionism: Myths, Politics and Scholarship in Israel* (London: Verso).

Quigley, John (1990) *Palestine and Israel: A Challenge to Justice* (Durham, NC: Duke University Press).

—— (2005) *The Case for Palestine: An International Law Perspective* (Durham, NC: Duke University Press).

Qumsiyeh, Mazin B. (2004) *Sharing the Land of Canaan* (London: Pluto Books).

Rabkin, Yakov M. (2006) *A Threat From Within: A Century of Jewish Opposition to Zionism* (London: Zed Books).

Reinhart, Tanya (2006) *The Road Map to Nowhere* (London: Verso).

Rodinson, Maxime (2001) *Israel: A Colonial-Settler State?* (New York: Pathfinder Press).

Rose, N.A. (1973) *The Gentile Zionists: A Study in Anglo-Zionist Diplomacy, 1929–1939* (London: Routledge).

Roy, Sara (2001) 'Decline and disfigurement: the Palestinian economy after Oslo', in Roane Carey (ed.), *The New Intifada* (London: Verso) pp. 91–109.

Ruether, Rosemary Radford and Herman J. Ruether (2002) *The Wrath of Jonah* (Minneapolis, MN: Fortress Press).

Said, Edward W. (2000) *The End of the Peace Process* (London: Granta Books).

Sayigh, Rosemary (2007) *The Palestinians: From Peasants to Revolutionaries* (London: Zed Books).

Segev, Tom (1998) *1949: The First Israelis* (New York: Henry Holt and Company).

—— (2002) *One Palestine, Complete* (London: Abacus).

—— (2007) *1967: Israel, the War, and the Year that Transformed the Middle East* (London: Little, Brown).

Shafir, Gershon (2007) 'Zionism and colonialism', in Ilan Pappe (ed.), *The Israel/Palestine Question: A Reader* (Abingdon: Routledge) pp. 78–93.

Shearer, David and Anuschka Meyer (2005) 'The dilemma of aid under occupation', in Michael Keating, Anne Le More and Robert Lowe (eds), *Aid, Diplomacy and Facts on the Ground* (London: Royal Institute of International Affairs) pp. 165–76.

Shlaim, Avi (2000) *The Iron Wall* (New York: W.W. Norton).

—— (2007) 'The debate about 1948', in Ilan Pappe (ed.), *The Israel/Palestine Question: A Reader* (Abingdon: Routledge) pp. 139–60.

Smith, Charles D. (2004) *Palestine and the Arab-Israeli Conflict*, Fifth edn (Boston, MA: Bedford/St Martin's).

Stevens, Richard P. (1973) 'Smuts and Weizmann', *Journal of Palestine Studies*, Vol. 3, No. 1, pp. 35–59.

Sufian, Sandy and Mark LeVine (eds) (2007) *Reapproaching Borders: New Perspectives on the Study of Israel-Palestine* (Lanham, MD: Rowman & Littlefield Publishers Inc.).

Tekiner, Roselle (1988) 'The "Who is a Jew?" controversy in Israel: a product of political Zionism', in Roselle Tekiner, Samir Abed-Rabbo and Norton Mezvinsky (eds), *Anti-Zionism: Analytical Reflections* (Brattleboro, VT: Amana Books) pp. 62–89.

Thomas, Baylis (1999) *How Israel was Won: A Concise History of the Arab-Israeli Conflict* (Lanham, MD: Lexington Books).

Tilley, Virginia (2005) *The One-State Solution* (Michigan, MI: University of Michigan Press).

Tutu, Desmond (1984) *Hope and Suffering* (London: Fount Paperbacks).

Veracini, Lorenzo (2006) *Israel and Settler Society* (London: Pluto Press).

Vitullo, Anita (2005) 'The long economic shadow of the wall', in Michael Sorkin (ed.), *Against the Wall* (New York: The New Press) pp. 100–21.

Weizman, Eyal (2007) *Hollow Land* (London: Verso).

Will, Donald and Sheila Ryan (1990) *Israel and South Africa* (Trenton, NJ: Africa World Press).

Yiftachel, Oren (2002) 'The shrinking space of citizenship: ethnocratic politics in Israel', *Middle East Report*, No. 223, pp. 38–45.

Younis, Mona (2000) *Liberation and Democratization* (Minneapolis, MN: Minnesota University Press).

Zureik, Elia (1979) *The Palestinians in Israel: A Study in Internal Colonialism* (London: Routledge and Kegan Paul).

Index